The Wounded Attorney

The Wounded Attorney

How Psychological Disorders Impact Attorneys

Catherine Young and Wendy Packman

LEXINGTON BOOKS
Lanham • Boulder • New York • London

Published by Lexington Books
An imprint of The Rowman & Littlefield Publishing Group, Inc.

4501 Forbes Boulevard, Suite 200, Lanham, Maryland 20706
www.rowman.com
86-90 Paul Street, London EC2A 4NE

British Library Cataloguing in Publication Information Available

Library of Congress Cataloging-in-Publication Data

Names: Young, Catherine (Clinical psychologist), author. | Packman, Wendy,
author.
Title: The wounded attorney : how psychological disorders impact attorneys
/ Catherine Young and Wendy Packman.
Description: Lanham : Lexington Books, [2022] | Includes bibliographical
references and index. | Summary: "In The Wounded Attorney, authors Young
and Packman explore how mental health issues appear in the legal
profession by examining attorney disbarment records and arguing for a
therapeutic approach to attorney discipline that destigmatizes mental
health issues"-- Provided by publisher.
Identifiers: LCCN 2021055705 (print) | LCCN 2021055706 (ebook) | ISBN
9781793626462 (cloth) | ISBN 9781793626486 (paperback) | ISBN
9781793626479 (ebook)
Subjects: LCSH: Lawyers--United States--Discipline. | Lawyers--Mental
health--United States. | Lawyers--Mental health services--United States.
Classification: LCC KF308 .Y68 20220 (print) | LCC KF308 (ebook) | DDC
174/.30973--dc23/eng/20211203
LC record available at https://lccn.loc.gov/2021055705
LC ebook record available at https://lccn.loc.gov/2021055706

To all who serve the Law with dedication, dignity, and compassion.

Contents

List of Tables

Introduction

Wendy and I met in the fall of 2012 when I began my doctoral program in clinical psychology at Palo Alto University (PAU). I had just graduated from law school, moved to the Bay Area, and was temporarily living out of a hotel near Palo Alto. Wendy's ethics class was the first I attended on campus. I was thrilled to hear Wendy was a JD/PhD, a lawyer and a psychologist, when she introduced herself to the class. I immediately knew I wanted to work with her while in the program. We bonded over our shared miserable California bar exam study experiences, trading perplexing MBE questions, and rattling off haunting phrases like the rule against perpetuities. Wendy accepted me into her JD/PhD research group geared towards law and clinical psychology students in the PAU joint degree program. We met regularly to discuss viable research topics and discovered we had a common interest in studying disenfranchised populations, i.e., individuals who suffer and who may not be recognized in the mainstream research literature. Invisible people, we called them.

Invisibility is a common theme within mental health circles. It probably would not be too far of a stretch to say the majority of patients seen by mental health clinicians carry invisible wounds. Patients treated in outpatient mental health settings are frequently called the "walking wounded" and present with a range of problems: anxiety, depression, grief, trauma, and addiction to name a few. Some patients wait a long time before entering treatment; others come in the midst of a crisis. And some patients who never seek treatment remain invisible. Thus began our journey to studying attorneys, a population we viewed as highly interesting in terms of hidden and often untreated mental health issues.

Through our own experiences working in a variety of legal settings, we have seen attorneys suffer in silence. Between the two of us we have worked in several stressful law firms ranging from "Biglaw" corporations to solo firms and non-profit legal aids. Mental health issues were present and maybe even abundant; there were attorneys who were angry all the time, depressed, shouting, stressed, but tight-lipped about their problems. One attorney who Wendy worked with never showed up to work again after leaving a post-it note on their chair one day that simply said, "I'm done." Though a lot of lip service is paid to attorney well-being, meditation, and mindfulness, the law is still a dog-eat-dog world.

As both attorneys and psychologists, we are in a unique position to understand attorney culture and we are also able to apply a social scientist perspective for research. As researchers we desire to expand the literature on attorney mental health by drawing on published legal disciplinary cases, scholarly journal articles, law review articles, and academic books. We hope this book is useful to attorneys, law students, and mental health practitioners who may treat attorneys. Social scientists who study attorney populations may also find this book helpful.

Our goals in writing this book are multifaceted. We endeavor to destigmatize and normalize mental health issues for attorneys while providing information about how impairment affects attorneys. We want to discuss possible solutions to the mental health crisis within the field and explore alternatives to the traditional law firm model. We are also mindful of the climate in which this book is written and surmise a need for more support in the legal community. The onset of COVID-19 during the winter and spring months of 2020 upended legal operations across the nation, and at the time of this writing it is still unclear how attorneys will be affected in the long run although remote meetings over Zoom may be here to stay. It is in this vein that we aim to broaden the resources available to attorneys in a time where there is a potential for an increase in prolonged isolation, trauma, and grief.

We have divided the book into nine chapters. In chapter one we describe what it is like to work as an attorney to highlight the potential cracks in the system where mental health and substance use problems spring forth. Chapter two is a literature review for attorney mental health studies to date. We explain state bar disciplinary boards in chapter three and how they tend to inadvertently punish attorneys struggling with mental health and substance use issues. Disciplinary rules under the ABA's Model Rules for Lawyer Disciplinary Enforcement are used over individual state rules to provide a foundation in understanding the regulation of attorneys. In chapters four through six we highlight the more prevalent mental health issues afflicting attorneys by presenting exploratory data on reported mental health disorders using available state bar disciplinary records. To examine in further detail the kinds of mental health issues and outcomes attorneys encounter, we discuss real life case examples found in state bar disciplinary proceedings. We illustrate problems attorneys face using actual instances of mental health illnesses, substance use disorders, and co-morbid illnesses. In chapter seven we summarize our findings in light of what we know about attorney mental health and discuss overall trends in our data and recommendations for the legal community. In chapter eight we provide treatment and recommendations to attorneys as well as to mental health professionals who treat the legal community. Aside from talking about the benefits of mental health treatment, we describe various state and local programs aimed at helping attorneys. Lastly in chapter nine, we provide future recommendations for systemic changes within the legal profession.

As you read this book, we wish to note some things to keep in mind about our choice of words in the text. We prefer to use the term attorney to indicate a licensed law professional who offers legal advice to clients. This does not mean the term lawyer is in absentia; rather, lawyer will continue to be used when quoted by others or when necessary. The difference between attorney and lawyer may be negligible and the terms may in fact even be interchangeable, but we wish to maintain a consistency in our language if possible. Another practical matter is how we offer information from the fifth edition of the *Diagnostic and Statistical Manual of Mental Disorders* (DSM-5). We reference the DSM-5 (2013), the most current version of the DSM, when explaining mental health and substance use disorders. The criteria we describe may conflict with other resources you have if it was published using a previous version of the DSM.

Finally, we want to emphasize that this book is not intended to be used as legal or mental health advice or in place of treatment. Please consult with a trained mental health professional if you are experiencing mental health or substance use issues. As attorneys and mental health clinicians, we offer this disclaimer in earnest because we know there are many individuals in need who are looking for help. We urge you to take advantage of the available resources and wish you good health.

Chapter 1

The Realities of Practicing Law

Over the past several decades—in law firms across the US—employers have encouraged and even celebrated work habits which undermine the physical and mental health of employee associates though it was known within the legal profession that attorneys have unaddressed mental health needs and substance use problems. Unrealistic billing expectations, tight deadlines, and heavy volumes of work requiring attention to detail have created a culture of acceptable (and revered) workaholism. Often, this cyclical pattern of over-work and burnout results in many attorneys becoming vulnerable to brief and/or chronic mental health and substance use disorders that ultimately lead to referrals to state bars and even disciplinary actions. In this book, we want to highlight: 1) what mental health and substance use disorders actually look like in attorneys; and 2) how the judicial system including courts and state bars misinterpret those disorders.

Attorney work culture is unique in that it combines high stakes, intense pressure, and hostile work environments. The demands can be difficult to manage whether working in a large national law firm (aka "Biglaw") or as a solo practitioner. The following chapter describes the stresses that begin in law school, current attorney demographics, common jobs in the law, and their workload, stresses, and drawbacks to illustrate how an attorney may become susceptible to impairment.

LAW SCHOOL STRESS

In general, research has supported the theory that attending law school is a unique experience that can be detrimental to human health (Austin 2013; Rosen 2011). Unlike undergraduates, law students spend most of the three years it takes to earn their Juris Doctor degrees competing against each other (Kissam 1989). Law school can be a deeply humbling and even demoralizing path towards becoming an attorney which pre-law undergrads may not be prepared for.

It is true that many of the triggers and/or conditions for mental health issues in attorneys actually begin in law school where there is no end to stress. During the first year of law school, typically referred to as "1L," law students become oriented to a new landscape where they are told grades are everything and only the top of the class gets good-paying jobs or jobs at all.[1] An 1L from California who experienced problems related to depression and anxiety talked about the adjustment from undergraduate to law school: "In college, I felt like I was the big fish in a little pond, but in law school, I had become the little fish in a big ocean. . . My mind kind of just snapped. It was a very dark period. . ." (Karabin 2015). Rankings, a type of "peer-to-peer stigmatization" (Rosen 2011, 178) play a significant role in the indoctrination of law students to the profession in that students begin to associate a higher rank to something better and more prestigious (Flanagan 2008). The perception of prestige applies to a multitude of scenarios in a law students' career: which law school to attend (preferably within the top 15 of the first tier), what rank they are in the class (top 10 percent is best) (Rosen 2011), whether to participate on law review (becoming an editor or the Editor-in-Chief is the goal), whether to complete a clerkship (federal clerkships preferred with the goal of clerking for a Supreme Court Justice), how many job interviews they are offered during On Campus Interviews (the more, the better), where students intern over their 2L summer (preferably at a large law firm that will offer a job upon graduation), and sometimes even how many hours they log in the law library (Bowers 2010). It goes without saying that the constant pressure of doing as much as possible to get ahead in a competitive environment is the norm.

It may be unsurprising to learn then that recent studies on law school students have yielded quite dismal findings when it comes to mental health and substance use issues. For example, out of over 300 law school students in one study, almost half of the participants met the threshold for anxiety while more than half of the sample met the threshold for depression (Flynn, Li, and Sánchez 2019). Studies conducted internationally show similar results where it has been reported that about a third of law students experience high to very high psychological distress (Kelk et al. 2009) and could likely meet criteria for depression (Rabkow et al. 2020). In a study conducted at a Midwestern law school, researchers found that 20.4 percent of law school students reported being diagnosed with a mental health disorder while 15 percent reported thinking they may have a drinking problem (Reed et al. 2016). Additionally, almost a fifth of the law school students in the sample reported driving under the influence of alcohol or drugs within the past year leading up to the survey (Reed et al. 2016). To complicate things further, researchers have found positive correlations between and among anxiety, stress, and depression in law students, meaning that students who experience one of these conditions tend to be more prone to experiencing the other two (Skead and Rogers 2014).

Prior research has also shown that law students tend to underutilize counseling resources (Gutierrez 1985) which, in light of more recent studies, appears to in part be related to stigma (Organ, Jaffe, and Bender 2016). When asked whether they would seek help for mental health-related issues, law students reported fears that seeking treatment may interfere with their entry into the profession. In one study, over 65 percent of the law students expressed concerns that seeking help for mental health would affect their career while almost 10 percent said in fact they would not seek help at all for mental health-related issues in the future (Reed et al. 2016). These results paralleled another study from 2016 finding an overwhelming majority of law students believed that seeking help for substance use or mental health issues could impede their admission to the bar or their ability to obtain a job (Organ et al. 2016). In fact, almost half of the students from this sample reported thinking they would have a better chance of getting admitted to the bar if their mental health or substance use problem remained hidden (Organ et al. 2016). These studies indicate that a significant amount of law students may need professional help but are hesitant to reach out.

One common reason as to why students may not seek help which appears to be reinforced by law school culture is minimization or denial of problems, especially when their grades are satisfactory. As one attorney who currently described herself as an alcoholic reflected on her problems with drinking, "I graduated from law school in the top 5 percent of my class. Drinking didn't affect my school performance, so why would I question the amounts I drank?" (Also Inside 2007, 184). The ability to achieve good grades could therefore falsely imply a lack of pathology, as if grades were a barometer of law school student health. But as we are aware, students who are in denial may not recognize they already have a problem or could be on the path to developing more serious psychopathology later on in their careers.

In a kind of chicken-or-the-egg argument, opinions on whether students or the law school educational environment are to blame seem split when it comes to mental health issues. In fact, it is not uncommon for scholars to ascribe blame on both ends. While some have referred to law school as a "hotbed of depression" (Temple 2012, 1) that "destroy[s] law students' gifts" (Jolly-Ryan 2009, 124), others have theorized it is the law school admissions committees who select more pathologically-inclined students (Danmeyer and Nunez 1999). This theory of blaming incoming law students for their problems does not seem to hold water, though, since studies and literature on the topic have demonstrated students entering law school experience a decline in functioning over the course of law school (Benjamin, Darling, and

Sales 1990; Jones 2015; Reed et al. 2016; Reifman, McLntosh, and Ellsworth 2001; Shapcott, Davis, and Hanson 2018). Even still, both law students and attorneys alike have been described as "notoriously depressive" individuals who are defensively pessimistic and, in fact, better equipped[2] for the legal field due to their depressive predispositions (Felder 2014, 66). From what we know about human physiology, however, chronically increased levels of stress and cortisol can lead to a host of health problems including headaches, fatigue, high blood pressure, digestive issues, sleep disorders, depression, and anxiety (Robinson 2020). While stress might appear to be somewhat beneficial in the short-term for legal training, it is quite harmful in the long-run for overall health.

CHARACTER AND FITNESS TESTS

Ever since the U.S. Supreme Court case *In re Griffiths* (1973) established that states have a constitutional interest in deciding whether attorney applicants possess "the character and general fitness requisite for an attorney and counselor," state bars began incorporating what most states refer to as the Character and Fitness evaluation or the "moral application." The Character and Fitness evaluation is yet another step in the process towards becoming an attorney and can generally be thought of as a thorough background investigation where the idea is to screen applicants for mental health issues that could negatively impact their capacity to practice law. Applicants carry the burden of proving by clear and convincing evidence they have good moral character and are expected to answer all questions in the evaluation with candor (Hudson 2016). As with any background investigation, state bars can take months to investigate Character and Fitness applicants even when everything goes smoothly, so delays can hinder entry into the profession.

Under the National Conference of Bar Examiners' (NCBE) Comprehensive Guide to Bar Admission Requirements (2021), "evidence of mental or emotional instability" and "evidence of drug or alcohol dependency" are listed as relevant conduct subject to further inquiry. In line with the NCBE, most state bars ask applicants for information regarding current mental health conditions on their Character and Fitness tests[3] with Florida, Kentucky, and Texas going a step further by asking specifically about whether an applicant has had Bipolar Disorder, Schizophrenia, and/or depression (American Bar Association 2020d). In addition to querying mental health and addiction history, some state bars ask whether applicants have asserted a mental health disorder or condition as part of a defense in past disciplinary actions[4] (American Bar Association 2020d). Several articles have criticized the Character and Fitness evaluation's purpose and methods and call for further exploration into alternative methods of evaluating applicants (Levin 2014; Levin, Zozula, and Siegelman 2015) or complete elimination altogether of questions regarding mental health (Clow 2020).

For many applicants, the Character and Fitness evaluation can be an intrusive examination into past mental health and addiction history that could result in employment setbacks. In the past, applicants who endorsed questions on mental health and/or substance use were subjected to additional scrutiny and/or even blocked from being admitted to the bar.[5] State bars prevented such applicants from admission due to the belief that a history of mental health or substance use issues constituted behavior that would negatively impact the applicant's ability to practice law. Accordingly, some scholars have questioned the constitutionality of Character and Fitness questions.[6] There has been a history of discrimination alleged by law students against state bars who feel that asking sensitive questions about mental health history should not prevent an individual from being admitted to practice law, which has resulted in bar examiners amending application questions (Banta 1995) and the Department of Justice issuing regulatory guidelines (Clow 2020; Persky 2014). In practice, research has shown that while being diagnosed with a mental health disorder or being treated for a mental illness was associated with a higher chance of discipline, a past history of substance use and/or treatment for substances did not increase the chance of being disciplined (Herr 1997).

The perception that endorsing a history of these issues could lead to problems with bar admission, however, persists and contributes to ongoing stigma regarding mental health and substance use. In a sample of over 1,300 Character and Fitness applicants from Connecticut, for example, researchers found that only about 3 percent of the applicants, or what we would deem as well below the standard prevalence rates in the general population, reported problems with either a mental or emotional disorder and/or substance use (Levin, Zozula, and Siegelman 2015). These results indicate a strong bias towards underreporting mental health conditions and conflict with prevalence studies revealing higher-than-average rates of mental health and substance use disorders in attorneys.

ATTORNEY DEMOGRAPHICS

Attorneys worked in a variety of settings throughout the US and held 823,900 jobs nationwide in 2018 (Bureau of Labor Statistics 2020). As of 2020, the ABA reported the states with the largest number of active attorneys on their rolls were New York (184,662), California (168,569), Texas (92,833), and Florida (79,328) (American Bar Association 2020c). Approximately 48 percent of all attorneys were employed in legal services, 20 percent were self-employed, and 18 percent worked for local, state, or federal government (Bureau of Labor Statistics 2020).

According to the U.S. Bureau of Labor Statistics, the median pay for all attorneys in 2019 was $122,960 per year; however, this figure is a bit misleading because about half of all attorney salaries fell between $40,000 and $70,000. Salaries for attorneys reflected a bimodal distribution representing the public and private sectors respectively with one peak at around $50,000 and a second larger peak at around $190,000 for a mean salary of $98,150 (National Association for Law Placement 2018b). Public sector jobs tend to pay far less than their private sector counterparts and start at around $48,000 (National Association for Law Placement 2018a). First-year associates at large law firms are able to command salaries at the $190,000 mark in markets such as New York City, D.C., Dallas, and Southern California.

DIVERSITY AMONG ATTORNEYS

Demographically, attorneys as a group suffer from an overall lack of diversity. As recently as 2020, states that track gender continued to record individuals as either male or female, with attorneys who identify as male accounting for approximately 63 percent of the population (American Bar Association 2020b). With respect to LGBT individuals, only about 4 percent of law firm associates and 2 percent of law firm partners identify as LGBT (National Association for Law Placement 2019). Astonishingly, attorneys with disabilities make up one-half of one percent (National Association for Law Placement 2019) though nationally it is estimated 1 in 4 adults in the U.S. live with some type of disability (Centers for Disease Control and Prevention 2020).

Although most state bars do not log information about race and ethnicity, the majority of attorneys (86 percent) who were surveyed identify as White (American Bar Association 2020b). Hispanic and African-American attorneys appear to be significantly underrepresented, accounting for a combined total of about 10 percent of attorneys at 5 percent each (American Bar Association 2020b). The number of attorneys of color has increased in law firms throughout the past decade, yet firms situated in the Midwest such as Indianapolis, Cleveland, and Cincinnati remain less diverse than firms located in metropolitan areas like Miami and Los Angeles (American Bar Association 2020g).

TYPES OF ATTORNEYS/LAW FIRMS

Biglaw and Firm Attorneys

Law firms are the most common employment environment for attorneys. Though much of our culture in the US stereotypes the attorney as working at a large law firm in Biglaw, in reality only about 20 percent of all private practice attorneys work in a large law firm of 100 or more employees (O'Connell 2019). The majority of attorneys employed in firms work in small firms of about 10 lawyers or less.

Law firms are generally set up as a tiered hierarchy system with senior staff at the top directing the mid- and early-career attorneys. Managing partners at the top of the food chain ensure the firm runs smoothly and manage the daily business operations involved in generating profits. Attorneys who become law firm partners are shareholders of the firm who have been promoted after several years of meeting billing requirements (more on billing later) with the firm. Finally, the law firm associates are generally younger attorneys, some of whom have recently graduated, who work as employees of the firm and have not yet made partner. Junior associates therefore end up doing much of the grunt work within the firm.

For some young attorneys working in Biglaw, the culture within the firm can act as insulation against real problems outside of the office. One anonymous attorney who reflected on her past stated:

> I got a job as an associate. . . It seemed as if I had finally made it. . . I was making more money than I ever had. Partying was a part of my life. I had a car accident while in a blackout, but no one was injured so I quickly dismissed the event as something that could happen to anyone. I never thought I had a problem. (Also Inside 2007, 184)

Problems may be well-hidden since law firms are notorious for requiring staff to work well beyond the typical 40-hours-a-week business model. Some associates work upwards of 70 to 80 hours a week. Yale Law School (2018) estimated that a standard full-time law firm job would require working almost 10 and a half hours a day Monday–Friday for an entire year with no sick days off. It is not uncommon for law firms to expect an attorney's personal life to take a back seat to professional obligations. As one transactional lawyer put it, the negotiations involved in corporate law "often results in extremely long hours. And as a deal moves toward its closing, it becomes an exercise in stamina as much as skillful negotiation. . ." (Kim 2011, 26). The same attorney went on to add a sobering thought that "[a] big part of 'biglaw' (or megafirm) life is canceling plans, and you learn to get pretty good at it. . ."

(30). Thus, it is perhaps expected that law firm duties would take precedence over having a personal life.

Although the concept of a work-life balance is promoted within law firms, in truth many attorneys are unable to make it work. Work deadlines, client demands, and frequent requests from management to work past quitting time all make having a life outside of law difficult. This is especially true for any associates in the prime years of their life who dream of making partner. Finding time to socialize with friends, recharge, date, or even have a family can prove challenging. Women attorneys in particular are susceptible to having their careers cut short when they are forced to juggle pursuing law firm partnership and motherhood. Erin Johnston (2018), litigation partner at Kirkland & Ellis, wrote: "I distinctly remember early in my career asking for yet another leave of absence just after returning from maternity leave, and my mind was flooded with thoughts about how my circumstances just didn't fit with a career in BigLaw."

SOLO PRACTITIONERS

Solo attorneys who "hang out a shingle" also experience a great deal of stress. In essence, solo attorneys function as manager, law firm partner, and associate all in one. Solos have the responsibility of taking care of all the legal services they provide as well as managing the business of being an attorney. Solos have a lot of latitude as they can choose which clients and how much work to take on; but, this freedom comes with a cost as they can easily work 80- to 90-hour weeks. One private DUI defense lawyer noted, "Seldom does a day go by, including Saturday and Sunday, that I don't take and make phone calls to clients or do some work" (Kim 2011, 281). He further said that, similar to Biglaw attorneys, his personal life had suffered due to having to frequently cancel plans with his wife.

Solo attorneys who are less fortunate when it comes to generating business have added stress when faced with underemployment and unemployment concerns. Without a safety net of a larger firm to draw clients from, solo attorneys are vulnerable to experiencing significant mental health burdens depending on how the legal services market is doing. A former solo attorney named "Eric" who described his law practice as "tanking" said that during his more difficult times he even experienced suicidal ideation (Goswamy 2019, 66).

Unfortunately, some solo attorneys working in today's post-COVID-19 world may be headed towards the same obstacles Eric endured. With unemployment in the US at their highest rates during the pandemic (Congressional Research Service 2021), it is likely that many individuals will not have the means and/or choice to hire a private attorney. Also, fewer clients mean less income for solo attorneys which can in turn lead to shuttered offices. One North Carolina solo attorney commented that the slowdown in her work has been significant: "We have really gone from 90 miles per hour to maybe 10" (Boughton 2020). While it still remains to be seen how the pandemic affects the legal market, it is clear that many solo attorneys will struggle to stay afloat. To make matters worse, solo and small practice attorneys, who make up the majority of attorney disciplinary cases, are at increased risk of receiving complaint notices from the state bar.

GOVERNMENT AND PUBLIC SECTOR ATTORNEYS

Attorneys who work for the government and/or public sector not only experience demanding workloads, but also are paid a fraction of what Biglaw associates earn. Government and public sector attorneys can include prosecutors, public defenders, administrators, and public interest advocates, all of whom often have to stretch themselves thin. Government and public sector attorneys frequently end up multitasking through weekends and vacations depending on the needs of the agency. As one prosecutor named "Walter" said, "This job is great for people with ADD (Attention Deficit Disorder). . . because doing six things at once is usually the order (norm) of the day" (Kim 2011, 41). It can get so busy at the agency that physical needs such as hunger are compromised. Walter added, "While I usually try to eat lunch, the flow of the day often dictates if and when I eat. I have found that if you drink copious amounts of coffee, you will not feel hungry" (43).

On the other side of the court, state public defenders in the past have been so burdened with work they refused to take on additional cases and have even sued agencies to restrict the number of defendants they are assigned (Eckholm 2008). Public defenders commonly deal with underfunding, budget cuts, and enormous caseloads teetering on the brink of unethical representation, but little has been done to address the inequities within the public defense model (let alone the criminal justice system as a whole). Criminal justice expert and law professor Norman Lefstein described the state of public defender work as "absolutely deteriorating" (Eckholm 2008) and opined it has likely led to questionable outcomes as more seasoned attorneys quit, leaving newer, less experienced attorneys to handle ever-increasing caseloads.

For some like law professor-turned-Administrative Judge Brian Clarke who first experienced depression in college before relapsing in law school and then again after the birth of his children, the demands of work often encroach on personal life and create a tug-of-war of guilt where no one wins. He explained:

I wanted to be the perfect lawyer, husband, and father. No matter what I did, I felt overwhelmed and guilty. If I spent time with my family, I felt badly about not being in the office and vice versa. . . . I was always anxious and terrified of making a mistake or letting someone down. I didn't know how to deal with this, so I tried to ignore it. Eventually, I started doing things that were out of character like not returning phone calls or emails. . . . I was very close to taking my own life at that point. (Clarke 2014)

Judge Clark's illuminating admissions reveal how negative feelings can easily snowball into much more serious and acute issues such as suicidal ideation which often necessitate mental health treatment.

ATTORNEY DUTIES

The Nightmare of Billable Hours

In *The New Billable Hour* (2019, 19), California attorney Ritu Goswamy keenly observed:

How can you take any time to relax when there is barely enough time to meet your billable-hours requirement?. . . This billable-hour system sets you up to fail. You cannot see time in the same way. Your time is not yours and it is not really even time. It is this idea that your worth is measured in time. . .

Billable hours accounts for the "single biggest complaint" (Alfini and Van Vooren 1995, 63) and the largest toll on attorneys' personal lives (Fortney 2000). Attorneys working in law firms bill clients for time spent working on cases, i.e., billable hours. Billable hours are actually divided into six-minute increments, not hours, so attorneys who maintain logs are responsible for keeping track of all their time down to the minute. Unfortunately, as Ms. Goswamy alluded to, many attorneys equate their earned billable hours to self-worth, meaning the more hours one puts in at the office, the more valuable they feel they are to the firm and within the profession.

Law firms are well-known for requiring staff to work long hours so they can bill more, and many attorneys work well over the standard 40-hour work week to meet their firm's billing requirements. Billable hour requirements generally range from 1,500 to 2,500 hours annually with about a third of attorneys (32.1 percent) working at least 2,200 hours per year (National Association for Law Placement 2016). Attorneys must reach their billing goals to earn their base salary, so the junior associate making a $190,000 annual salary is likely making far less per hour than you might assume after calculating their total time spent in the office. At some firms, a 50- to 80-hour work week is the norm. In fact, more than 60 percent of attorneys working in the largest law firms (defined as more than 700 attorneys in firm size) billed for 2,200 or more hours in the year 2014 (National Association for Law Placement 2016). Conversely, the majority of attorneys (58.3 percent) in smaller firms (defined as 100 or fewer attorneys) billed on average between 1,000 and 1,999 hours (National Association for Law Placement 2016). Thus, the larger the law firm, the more billable hours are required.

One of the reasons billable hours have such a bad reputation is that they simply are not an accurate reflection of the amount of actual time worked. The billable hour is, in fact, a lie because attorneys spend much more time working on client matters than what they are able to bill for. For example, an attorney who works a 12-hour day may only be able to bill for five of those hours if the rest are not spent providing direct services to clients (Goswamy 2019). Even worse, in an effort to avoid being accused of overbilling (aka "padding the bill") or to appear as if they did not spend as much time work-ing on a project, some attorneys end up underbilling for the amount of time they worked. Underbilling or underestimating billable hours, as you might imagine, results in a vicious cycle where attorneys are forced to make up for inadequate billable hours by working more, resulting in what Fortney (2000, 241) referred to as a "time famine."

TOO MUCH WORK

Unsurprisingly, the most common reason identified for stress is having too much to do and not enough time to accomplish everything (Simmons 2015). It seems as if no matter the area of law practice, attorneys are overwhelmed by the amount of work they have. A survey on attorney stress showed that over 60 percent of private attorneys reported feeling stressed most or all of the time at their job (Rodriguez 2018). Amongst judges, a lengthy docket of cases and working at length without a break were listed as the second and seventh sources of stress at work respectively (Swenson et al. 2020). Long hours at the office spent working on client matters ultimately means less time to relax and engage in self-care.

A host of possible mental health issues are associated with being over-worked, including feeling more stressed. Anxiety, depression, and addiction issues are just the tip of the iceberg for overworked attorneys. As a way of managing stress levels at the office, one German law firm even created an app with a panic button that attorneys can activate when they feel overworked to let colleagues know they are unable to take on another assignment (Simmons 2018). Law firm staff are able to see a rank order list of who is available for more work, i.e., who has not pushed the panic button. In the past, a concept such as a panic button would have likely been shunned at a law firm given how unyielding and cutthroat the legal market used to be. Any attorney who declined work would have likely been viewed as non-partner material or a poor fit for the firm. In today's society, however, perhaps a panic button could be a useful tool to streamline workflow and identify staff who need more support.

NETWORKING RESPONSIBILITIES: OPPORTUNITIES FOR MORE WORK

Networking functions can serve to connect individuals, but the pressure to network can feel like yet another obligation. In fact, up to 30 percent of an attorney's day could be spent networking (Schwartz 2010), and even when not networking, attorneys are trained to look for opportunities during informal meetings for meals or coffee breaks, through collaborative work in committees, or by written communication (Miano 2015). Law firms and bar associations often hold networking events where members are expected to socialize with colleagues to increase their chances of finding potential clients. Networking is such an integral aspect to attorney work that numerous ABA articles are devoted to troubleshooting barriers to networking. As one corporate transactional attorney said, "In a client-driven business such as ours, it is important that we build our network extensively. You never know who can introduce you to someone who might bring business to the firm, and a lot of the power of who you are rests in whom you know" (Kim 2011, 24).

The pressure to network can also lead to unintended consequences such as drinking problems. Booze is a staple at network events (perhaps it is even the main draw), and some attorneys may end up inadvertently developing, or accelerating, a substance use problem through merely attending a social work function. In response to this issue, the ABA's Task Force recommended in 2017 that networking events "deemphasiz[e] alcohol" (Woods 2018, 19).

EFFECTS ON ATTORNEYS

Secondary Traumatic Stress, Vicarious Trauma, and Compassion Fatigue

Attorneys can be exposed to and manifest effects of trauma in a variety of ways through their work with clients. Three types of distinct yet interrelated reactions to trauma that may apply to attorneys are secondary traumatic stress, vicarious trauma, and compassion fatigue. Secondary traumatic stress refers to the flood of feelings an individual can experience when exposed to traumatic events witnessed by another (Newell and Gordon 2010; Robinson-Keilig 2014). Literature on vicarious trauma has emphasized shifts in an individual's way of thinking that can occur after exposure to a traumatic event is transmitted to them (McCann and Pearlman 1990), while compassion fatigue is defined as contact with traumatizing material that induces symptoms of and may even meet criteria for diagnosis of posttraumatic stress disorder (PTSD) (Gentry, 2002).

These types of reactions to trauma can occur when exposed attorneys absorb the emotional content of their clients' traumatic narratives. Attorneys who work closely with clients in distress, such as in the areas of criminal defense (Levin et al. 2012; Seamone 2014; Vrklevski and Franklin 2008), prosecution (Gomme and Hall 1995), immigration (Markham 2020), family law (Brobst 2014; Fines and Madsen 2007), juvenile law (Hazilla 2016), and the judiciary[7] (Flores et al. 2009; Chamberlain and Miller 2009; Resnick, Myatt, and Marotta 2011) are particularly susceptible to absorbing client trauma. Effects of trauma in attorneys has been shown to manifest as symptoms consistent with PTSD, depression, and burnout (Levin et al. 2011). It has been presupposed too that the COVID-19 pandemic will further compound existing trauma in many communities (Li et al. 2020).

For purposes of this book, we focus on compassion fatigue since as of 2018 it has been introduced as a mitigating factor (Bahn 2019; Rubin 2018).

BURNOUT

Burnout in particular often goes unnoticed as it is a gradual process that can start well before law school graduation. Burnout has been pathologized as a "syndrome of emotional exhaustion, depersonalization, and reduced personal accomplishment" (Maslach 1976) and a "disease of disengagement" by attorney and Stress & Resilience Institute founder Paula Davis-Laack which results in less productivity and enjoyment with work (Mangan 2015). Every part of an attorney's career ranging from the Socratic method taught in law school to the lack of ability to choose one's own clients has been theorized to contribute to burnout (Norton et al. 2016), although the origins of the condition have been hypothesized to be linked to insensitive parenting and a bias towards masochism (Berger 2000). Some attorneys who labor under the anxious belief that "people's problems don't stop just because it's a holiday" may not even allow themselves to enjoy a recuperative day off (Barrett 2017).

Former president of the New York Society of Clinical Psychologists and psychoanalyst Dr. Freudenberger who coined the phrase *burn out* noted that it was "virtually impossible" (19) for underachievers to burnout and that it was primarily an overachiever malady (Freudenberg and Richelson 1980). Individuals who burnout, according to Freudenberger and Richelson (1980), often end up turning to substances to cope and "may be cranky, critical, angry, rigid, resistant to suggestions, and given to behavior patterns that turn people off." In other words, burnout can lead to problems with addiction and alienation from others which can result in poor mental health outcomes.

Suffice it to say, the seeds for emotional distress are sown as early as 1L year in law school and thereafter throughout the practice of law. In some individuals, these seeds may unfortunately germinate and blossom into dysfunctional maladaptive coping, or later disciplinary action. In the next chapter we highlight research on attorney mental health before delving into the process of disciplinary actions. As we will show in the following chapters, the effects of stress in attorneys have been shown to manifest as symptoms consistent with mental health issues including anxiety and depressive disorders and/or substance use.

NOTES

1. Kissam (1989, 480) separated law students into "winners" (the top of the class), "journeymen" or "role players" (the middle of the pack), and "losers" (the bottom of the class).

2. Felder (2014) argues that a depressive predisposition makes an attorney work harder towards goals and therefore results in more success.

3. The following states ask about mental health conditions: AL, AK, AR, CO, CT, DE, DC, FL, GA, HI, ID, IN, IA, KS, KY, LA, ME, MD, MI, MN (2 years), MO, MT, NE, NV, NH, NJ, NM, NY, NC, ND, OH, OK, OR, RI, SC, SD, TX, UT, VT, WV, and WY. Many states ask if applicants have had mental health conditions within the past three years. On the longer end, MI asks if applicants have ever had any of the conditions asked about while NV asks if applicants had any of the conditions within the past 10 years. States which do not ask about mental health history include AZ, IL, MA, MS, PA, TN, VA, and WA.

4. These states include: AL, AR, CO, DE, DC, GA, HI, ID, IN, IA, KY, LA, ME, MD, MN, MO, MT, NE, NH, NM, NC, ND, OK, OR, RI, SD, TX, VT, WV, WI, and WY. The typical year range for this question is generally within the past 5 years but can be as little as two years or up to at any time in the applicant's life.

5. In Doe v. Kentucky (2020), U.S. District Judge Justin R. Walker compared the state bar admissions board to a drug cartel after Jane Doe alleged ADA violations against the KY Bar for holding up her license due to positive questions on her Character and Fitness application. Judge Walker determined she lacked standing to bring the suit but noted that in the future "[s]ome. . . plaintiffs will have standing to seek prospective relief. And when they do, the Bar Bureaucracy will have to answer for a medieval approach to mental health that is as cruel as it is counterproductive" (Doe 2020, 4).

6. See Averitt (2004) who argues that state bars that prevent applicants from being admitted based upon psychological problems disclosed in the Character and Fitness evaluation are in violation of substantive and procedural due process rights.

7. Similar to attorneys, judges reported work-related stress resulted in fatigue, problems with sleep, attention difficulties, ruminating or worrying, health concerns, and feeling anxious (Swenson et al., 2020). Almost 30 percent of judges reported that handling cases involving trauma was a significant source of on-the-job stress (Swenson et al., 2020). The stress of decision-making and the thought of issuing bad rulings has been shown to weigh on judges (Chamberlin and Miller 2009; Resnick et al. 2011).

Chapter 2

Research: Discipline and Attorney Psychological Problems

Statistical rates of mental health and/or substance use problems resulting in negative professional outcomes for attorneys are shockingly high. It has been estimated that anywhere from 50 percent to more than 80 percent of attorney discipline cases involve psychological distress or substance use (Heil 1993; Bloom and Wallinger 1988; Pregenzer 1993). The effects of attorney mental illness are felt by the client who indirectly suffers—statute of limitations lapse, pleadings go unfiled, default judgments are entered, appearances are missed, and cases go unprosecuted (Klingen 2002). However, despite the high correlation with mental illness, substance use, and disciplinary proceedings, the legal profession has made meager attempts to address the systemic underlying issues that give rise to these problems. In this chapter, we highlight the relevant empirical literature devoted to attorney mental illness and substance use to better understand the nature of the problem.

PREVALENCE RATES OF PSYCHOLOGICAL DISTRESS AND SUBSTANCE USE

General Population vs. Attorneys

Prevalence rates illustrating psychological distress or substance use within the attorney population generally point to higher rates than seen in the general US population. Attorneys have been estimated to experience depression and substance use disorders at higher rates than the average non-attorney. To put an illness such as depression into perspective, consider that the annual prevalence rates for Major Depressive Disorder—what most clinicians would consider "depression"—in the US is estimated to be 7.8 percent (National Alliance on Mental Illness, 2021) and may be three times higher for individuals between the ages of 18 and 29 (American Psychiatric Association

2013). Additionally, the Substance Abuse and Mental Health Services Administration (SAMHSA) estimated in 2018 that 7.3 percent (2.2 million) of adult individuals in the US had a substance use disorder, 16.2 percent (4.8 million) had a mental illness, and 3.6 percent (1.1 million) had both a substance use disorder and a mental illness.

In a 1990 Johns Hopkins study (Eaton et al. 1990) looking at a total of 104 occupations, however, researchers concluded that the occupation with the highest prevalence rate for depression was lawyer. Another 1990 study conducted by the North Carolina Bar Association found that 37 percent of attorneys surveyed admitted to being depressed, 25 percent reported physical symptoms of depression, and more than 11 percent endorsed suicidal ideation at least one to two times per month within the past year (Tarascio 2020). This same study also reported that 17 percent of attorneys drank between three and five alcoholic beverages a day. Several estimates state that rates of depression and drug use are twice as prevalent in attorneys than in the general population (Benjamin, Darling, and Sales 1990; Goldberg 1990).

Unfortunately, research on attorney prevalence rates are likely to be even higher than what is reported because of emotional defense mechanisms such as denial or lack of insight into illness. Denial has been described as a constant in addiction literature and tends to lead to flat-out rejection of problems or at the very least minimizing or dismissing (Heil 1993). Denial can play a role in mental illness where the attorney negates any suggestion that he/she is suffering; a lack of insight or awareness into deeper psychological issues may also be at play. Therefore, studies surveying a significant number of attorneys may not portray the entire picture of distress going on within the individual and might be better treated as general indicators of trends.

RESEARCH ON IMPAIRMENT

Possibly the most well-known modern study in the U.S. for its scope of surveying thousands of attorneys across many states is the 2016 landmark research project from researchers Patrick Krill, Ryan Johnson, and Linda Albert with support from the ABA Commission on Lawyer Assistance Programs (CoLAP) and nationally recognized treatment provider the Hazelden Betty Ford Foundation. Krill et al. (2016) anonymously sampled 12,825 attorneys from 19 US states. Most participants were married White individuals who had litigation experience and had used alcohol within the past 12 months (Krill et al. 2016). Out of the sample, a whopping 11,278 attorneys scored at a problematic drinking level on the AUDIT-C and 36.4 percent had scores within the hazardous drinking or alcohol use disorder categories (Krill et al. 2016).

The most common mental health illnesses reported by attorneys in the study were: anxiety, depression, social anxiety, ADHD, panic disorder, and bipolar disorder. Specifically, attorneys were assessed for and found to be struggling with significant rates of depression (28 percent), anxiety (19 percent), and stress (23 percent) within the sample (Krill et al. 2016). Of the 28 percent who endorsed depression, most individuals were assessed as experiencing moderate, severe, or extremely severe depression (Krill et al. 2016). In looking back on the study, Krill (2018) noted that "the problem with attorney depression is even worse than the numbers first sound" (11), which appears to be a fitting statement given that more than 10 percent of the attorneys in the study endorsed having suicidal ideation during their career (Krill et al. 2016).

Several other themes emerged surrounding substance use—younger attorneys reported more problem drinking than older attorneys; and people who were newer to the field were associated with more alcohol use than individuals who had been working longer (Krill et al. 2016). Attorneys in junior and senior level positions had higher proportions of drinking than other positions (Krill et al., 2016). Interestingly, 43.7 percent of the lawyers sampled felt like their alcohol use became a problem within 15 years of graduating from law school (Krill et al. 2016). Researchers noted between 21 and 36 percent were considered problem drinkers based on their scores from the brief assessments used and that those who screened positive as problem drinkers had significantly higher levels of mental-health distress than their peers (Krill 2016 as cited in Krill 2018). The two main barriers to substance use treatment were not wanting others to find out and concerns about confidentiality (Krill et al. 2016).

Following the ABA/Hazelden study, there was a flurry of activity within the ABA indicating that the organization was working on the problems raised in the research. The ABA CoLAP in conjunction with the National Organization of Bar Counsel (NOBC) and the Association of Professional Responsibility Lawyers (APRL) established the National Task Force on Lawyer Well-Being[1] ("Task Force") in 2016 (ABA 2018). The Task Force promoted awareness of mental health issues afflicting attorneys and introduced significant cultural changes surrounding mental illness and substance use within the profession, one of which was the presentation of a "well-being template" to be implemented in legal employment settings (ABA CoLAP 2019). Additionally, the Task Force proposed Resolution 105 aimed at improving the profession through creating action plans to address the findings from the ABA/Hazelden study (ABA Resolution 105, 2018). In 2017 the ABA also adopted Resolution 106 which requires attorneys to complete at least one hour of mental health or substance use continuing education units during every license renewal period.

Law schools too were pushed to make changes for students. The ABA House of Delegates in 2018 adopted nine total recommendations[2] focused on legal education while CoLAP began surveying and exploring law schools nationwide (Confino 2019). Results from CoLAP's inquiries showed that only about half (53 percent) of the 103 schools that responded had on-site mental health counselors, most schools (59 percent) did not offer any support groups for mental health or substance use disorders, and more than 93 percent percent omitted training on suicide prevention (Confino 2019).

Many states implemented changes following the ABA/Hazelden study (2016). For example, Mississippi and Kentucky established a Well Being Committee in January 2020; Oklahoma assembled a task force in 2019 and added additional ethics hour requirements to include mental health and substance use education; Minnesota held a well-being summit in 2019; South Dakota raised $30,000 for a pilot project for their Lawyer Assistance Program; Oregon held a wellness summit in 2019, began requiring an hour of MCLE on mental health/substance use/cognitive impairment, and is reevaluating its bar application questions on mental health history (Institute for Well-Being in Law 2021).

Since the ABA/Hazelden study (Krill et al. 2016) was published, critics have argued several points. The implications of the study, as some have found after thorough research, have been minimized to be "not as dire" as originally thought based on the lack of evidence showing bad outcomes (Edwards 2018). Because one would expect far worse outcomes as a result of high prevalence rates for mental health and/or substance use, the study has been criticized for sampling attorneys who are troubled by—but not necessarily directly impacted by—the topic of mental health and substance use (Edwards 2018; Velleman 2016). From this perspective, it is possible that the study includes a degree of self-selection bias, however, it would be problematic to deny the sheer number of study participants who actually did endorse such distressing data.

EMPIRICAL LITERATURE ON ATTORNEY MENTAL HEALTH

The concept of mental impairment affecting attorney work has been around since the late 1970s. In the Comment[3] section in *The Journal of the Legal Profession*, attorney Lee Hardegree (1979) discussed various legal cases across jurisdictions involving attorneys who were either barred from admission to the profession for admitting to mental health disorders or who attempted to use mental health issues as a way of mitigating disciplinary actions against them. Similarly, the American Bar Association (Skoler and

Klein 1979) tackled the issue of mental health impairment in disciplinary actions in their law review article where they referred to disciplining mentally ill attorneys as a "difficult problem" (228). The ABA analyzed the resulting outcomes of using mental incompetence as follows: no defense, a complete defense, and as a mitigating factor.

In 1984, Dr. Adam J. Krakowski, a physician from Champlain Valley Physicians Hospital in New York compared stress levels in a sample of 100 physicians and 50 attorneys. Using results analyzed from administering a structured interview, he found that physicians exhibited more compulsive behavior than their attorney counterparts. At the time of the study he noted that, in comparison to physicians, about half of the attorneys (46 percent) reduced their work during periods of stress, and attorneys reported experiencing depression at rates of only about a third of the prevalence rates reported by physicians. However, since Dr. Krakowski's study, further research has shown that attorneys demonstrate higher levels of mental illness such as depression than other professionals (Eaton et al. 1990), more psychological distress than pharmacists (Leignel et al. 2014), and potentially higher risk for burnout (Akhtar & Aydin 2019).

Instead of assessing for mental health, the ABA's Young Lawyers Division in 1985 surveyed attorney-participants on "job satisfaction" and found that 34 percent of the attorneys rated themselves as dissatisfied (Daicoff 2004). The ABA's initial study likely reflected a wake-up call for many about the worsening of attitudes towards lawyering. Similar results were reconfirmed in two follow-up studies the ABA conducted in the 1990s which showed that up to 43 percent of attorneys were in fact dissatisfied (Daicoff, 2004).

Though many researchers consider the ABA's surveys as one of the earliest studies on attorney mental health, Dr. G. Andrew H. Benjamin, a graduate of the JD/PhD program at the University of Arizona and pioneer researcher of attorney mental health, first presented results of a cross-sectional longitudinal study (1985) at the APA's 93rd Annual Convention. In his research, Dr. Benjamin compared symptoms indicative of psychopathology, or potential signs of mental disorder, to look at what, if any, potential impact law school had on a group of University of Arizona Law School students over time. He had a hunch based on "anecdotal literature," which was the only available evidence at the time, that the course of undergoing a legal education in fact impaired the individual's emotional well-being (Benjamin et al. 1985). He assessed student participants at three points in their legal careers: before they started law school, while they attended law school, and at post-graduation. What he found was that as law students continued through law school, their levels of psychopathology increased with no return to pre-law school levels after graduation (Benjamin et al. 1985). In other words, people who attended law school ended up with more mental health problems that did not go away once law school was over. The process of becoming an attorney, and not the experience of law school itself, was therefore correlated with higher mental disorders in these Arizona Law participants. The researchers concluded that law school had such a "pervasive socializing influence" on law students that they were in effect primed to develop psychopathology as they progressed from their pre-law years to 3L and beyond (Benjamin et al. 1985, 12).

One of the most popular attorney mental health studies cited is a 1990 University of Washington study looking at rates of depression, alcoholism, and cocaine use among 801 attorneys in the State of Washington. In this study, researchers sampled about 10 percent of the entire population of attorneys licensed in Washington. Results from this study indicated that 19 percent of Washington attorneys exhibited clinically significant levels of depression, 18 percent were "problem drinkers," and less than one percent used cocaine (Benjamin et al. 1990). For depression and alcohol use, researchers described the prevalence rates they discovered were approximately double as seen in the general population.

Another University of Washington study (Chiles 1990) compared smokers to nonsmokers. In a sample of 802 Washington attorneys, 614 men and 188 women, researchers found that attorneys who smoked cigarettes were far more likely than attorneys who did not smoke to report somatization, depression, anxiety, and problems with alcohol. Male smokers in particular were more likely to endorse somatization, obsessive-compulsiveness, depression, anxiety, phobic anxiety, paranoia, and psychotic symptoms (Chiles 1990). Attorneys who smoked were also found to endorse more feelings of anger and more likely to use alcohol (Chiles 1990). Further, the rates of being both depressed and having a problem with alcohol, labeled as "dual disordered" or "dual diagnosis," were more than three times for attorney smokers (13.1 percent) than attorney nonsmokers (4.1 percent). Perhaps in response to anecdotal information and data showing prevalence rates of alcoholism and other substances among attorneys, approximately 55 percent of state bars had developed programs or assembled committees to address substance use issues in attorneys and judges by the early 1990s (Human Rights 1992). Today that number is 100 percent and includes all US territories (Commission on Lawyer Assistance Programs 2020b).

In 1995 researchers at the University of Arizona and the University of Washington joined to study distress in attorneys with a focus on alcohol and psychological problems (Beck, Sales, and Benjamin 1995). By reviewing past datasets collected in earlier research, they compared their sample of Washington attorneys to their sample of Arizona attorneys at two years post-graduation.[4] The researchers described the attorneys in the samples as experiencing a "considerable amount of psychological distress" based on results obtained from assessments administered during these studies. Both male and female attorneys surveyed endorsed significantly more stress and anger than the normal population, and anger was found to be the most predictive variable in regards to distress (Beck et al. 1995). The researchers saw anger, a precursor to what they theorized as problematic drinking, as double-sided; on the one hand, "appropriately directed anger" (Beck et al. 1995, 57) was crucial to advocacy yet on the other hand it was thought of as harmful for those attorneys who were unable to disengage from work, i.e., workaholic attorneys.

INTERNATIONAL STUDIES ON
ATTORNEY MENTAL HEALTH

Across the pond, attorneys seem to fare no better when it comes to substance use. Solicitor and prolific writer of attorney substance use, Jonathan Goodliffe (1994), compared how authorities of disciplinary proceedings in England handled lawyer depression and alcohol use. Noting how much more robust U.S. case law appeared to be at the time regarding attorney impairment, Goodliffe (1994) recognized that the U.S. tended to employ check-in "monitors" for substance use (which England did not), and U.S. attorneys often claimed to be completely abstinent (vs. engaging in non-dependent use which may have been interpreted as nonproblematic in England where addiction is viewed as a symptom of an underlying problem). Finally, the mention of how alcohol use can trigger changes in affect, such as depressed mood, in English attorney discipline proceedings was relatively infrequent when compared to U.S. proceedings. Goodliffe (1994) chalked up some of these differences to the U.S. being more aware of how substance use and depression play a role in attorney work before expressing hope that the English courts would catch up with what is already happening within the profession.

Similarly, a study out of King's College London looked at how impairment related to alcohol use in male lawyers working in the U.K. (Brooke 1997). Impairment due to any substance, including widely-available alcohol, has been noted as being just as difficult to examine in the U.K. as it is in the U.S., and researchers commonly resort to pouring over archived disciplinary records in the Solicitors' Disciplinary Tribunal. In reviewing these disciplinary records, researchers noted that solicitors and barristers with alcohol problems reported high rates of several alarming professional consequences such as missed appointments/court hearings (51 percent), trouble with the police (48 percent), receiving warnings from employers/partners/clerks (41 percent), loss of driver's license due to drinking and driving (36 percent), loss of job/partnership/chambers (36 percent), loss of clients (34 percent), inability to meet fee targets (30 percent), inability to perform effectively in court (30 percent), and disciplinary proceedings (13 percent) (Brooke 1997).

Recent international studies have shown the number of attorneys reporting mental health issues during misconduct proceedings have increased. Australian university professors Baron and Corbin (2019) analyzed 10 years' worth of cases from 2008 to 2017 from eight Australian jurisdictions and found growth in case rates across all six states and two territories. From their review of the data, Baron and Corbin (2019) posited Australian disciplinary courts shared the following "guiding principles" (39) with respect to attorney misconduct cases and mental health: 1) the attorney must establish causation between their mental illness and misconduct; 2) submission of medical records; 3) psychologist evaluation reports are considered insufficient; 4) nonappearances by attorneys are viewed critically; and 5) mental illness does not excuse an attorney's misconduct. As you will see in upcoming chapters from our research, the results of Baron and Corbin's (2019) study parallel in many ways the attitudes of U.S. courts with respect to attorney mental health.

CURRENT STATE OF THE RESEARCH

Presently in the U.S., the ABA/Hazelden study (Krill et al. 2016) is seen as the benchmark in attorney mental illness and substance use research. Only time will tell how the study will change the landscape of attorney mental health but one outcome already appears clear: the ABA is attempting to once again acknowledge the issues of mental health and substance use in the legal profession. For now, the ABA/Hazelden study will more than likely follow in the footsteps of past empirical literature in that it will continue to be used as a reference point to show where we are with attorney mental health and substance use prevalence rates. Research on attorney mental health and substance use serves as a wake-up call to employers that their attorney workface is suffering, and has been suffering, for a long time. It will be interesting to see what changes are made within the next five, ten, or twenty years within the industry.

NOTES

1. As of 2020 the National Task Force on Lawyer Well-Being has become the Institute for Well-Being in Law. See https://lawyerwellbeing.net for more info.

2. The recommendations were: to create best practices for detecting and assisting students experiencing psychological distress, assess law school practices and offer

faculty education on promoting well-being in the classroom, empower students to help fellow students in need, include well-being topics in courses on professional responsibility, commit resources for on-site professional counselors, facilitate a confidential recovery network, provide education opportunities on topics related to well-being, discourage alcohol-centered social events, and conduct anonymous surveys relating to student well-being (Confino 2019).

3. Comments are frequently articles about legal cases of first impression and their impact (LexisNexis 2018).

4. The researchers examined how demographic variables correlated with distress. Aside from some age differences, no significant demographic variables were noted in the comparison but the investigators of the study identified that the Arizona attorneys had significantly higher measures for hostility and paranoid ideation whereas the Washington attorneys had significantly higher measures for interpersonal sensitivity and phobic anxiety according to scales on the Brief Symptom Inventory (BSI). For reference, the BSI is a 53-item self-report test normed on adult nonpatients that can be used to measure clinical outcomes and/or progress (Pearson, 2020).

Chapter 3

The Process of Attorney Discipline

Though attorney disciplinary actions in the U.S. date back to our legal origins in England and later the American colonies (Levin 2007), this book focuses on the modern era of attorney discipline. Much of what today's attorneys know about the current disciplinary system is based on the national attorney membership organization, the American Bar Association (ABA). In 1970, the ABA first adopted attorney discipline standards under the Clark Committee Report entitled *Problems and Recommendations in Disciplinary Enforcement* (American Bar Association 2020e). These standards were in effect until 1979 when the ABA began using the updated disciplinary standards published under the *Professional Discipline for Lawyers and Judges*. The standards were constructed to provide a structure in which lawyer discipline could be regulated (ABA, Model Rules preface 2020) and were in place until 1986 when the ABA approved the *Standards for Imposing Lawyer Sanctions* which provided for six different kinds of sanctions[1] (Kratovil 2000). In 1989 the ABA adopted the *Model Rules for Lawyer Disciplinary Enforcement* as a guide for states[2] in response to an evaluation they conducted on lawyer regulation (Levin 1998). The ABA's response galvanized states across the nation to roll out attorney disciplinary programs, and as a result, more state bars initiated their own disciplinary systems during this era. Clearer, more consistent criteria for regulation were implemented in an attempt to standardize attorney discipline. Today, all 50 states and US territories have a disciplinary system which is funded mostly through state bar dues or court fees.

As of the most recent survey on professional discipline, there were 83,073[3] complaints received on the more than 1,257,772[4] actively licensed attorneys in the U.S. (American Bar Association 2020a). Most complaints received were closed or dismissed after an investigation. This process of closing out cases is typical across states and throughout years. The number of cases resulting in an attorney being charged is always lower than the initial number of complaints received. For example, in the year 2019–2020 the State of Florida opened 3,557 cases and disciplined just 262 attorneys (The Florida

Bar 2021). This is pointed out not to minimize the seriousness of the cases that were charged but to note that the majority of cases filed against attorneys are closed or dismissed without formal charges.

State bars are responsible for licensing, regulating, and disciplining attorneys on the roll, but in general it is the highest state court that is responsible for meting out disciplinary actions (American Bar Association 2020e). Disciplinary actions can range from a letter of warning to disbarment. In between extremes there exists other forms of discipline, of course, such as private or public reproval, admonition, and private disciplinary sanction depending on the state. Much of a state's discipline program is not public and therefore accessible only through inquiry of an attorney's record. Aside from state courts, alternatives to discipline or diversion programs exist but not in every state. Reinstatement of an attorney license is possible if the attorney is disbarred, but this practice varies among states.[5]

THE PURPOSE OF DISCIPLINE

According to the ABA's *Model Rules for Lawyer Disciplinary Enforcement* (2020), the disciplinary system is not meant to punish but to deter unethical behavior. In addition to deterrence, state disciplinary bodies and law review articles note that the purpose of disciplining attorneys includes protecting the public and upholding professionalism (Rhode 1985). All three of the aforementioned goals tend to be used to suspend or disbar attorneys for, among other reasons, malfeasance, incompetence, and professional misconduct.

Although many state courts explicitly point to protecting the public in their opinions when disciplining attorneys, some have argued that courts tend to take on a more criminal law approach that serves more to punish than to protect (Zacharias 2003). Additionally, there is little evidence to date showing that individuals with mental health or substance use issues make poor attorneys. Given the reported elevated prevalence rates of psychological issues in the attorney population, it appears the vast majority of attorneys with these problems do not end up being disciplined (when comparing prevalence rates of problems in overall attorney population vs. prevalence rates in disciplined samples). Thus it would appear that sanctioning attorneys with mental health or substance use issues may not necessarily fulfill any of the goals disciplinary actions set out to accomplish.

REASONS FOR DISCIPLINE

The ABA Model Rules of Professional Conduct (Model Rules) set forth ethical guidelines and provides for circumstances when attorneys may be disciplined. The rules apply to all lawyers uniformly, regardless of any physical or mental health condition. Attorneys may be disbarred automatically for criminal convictions under Model Rule 8.4 and appear to be punished more harshly than other professionals.[6] Grounds for discipline include violating rules of professional conduct, willfully violating court orders or discipline, willfully failing to appear before disciplinary counsel, willfully failing to comply with subpoenas, or knowingly failing to respond to demands (American Bar Association 2020f). According to Model Rule 9, attorneys have a duty to cooperate with the disciplinary counsel and its investigations but still maintain their constitutional rights against self-incrimination and due process (American Bar Association 2020f). The most common reasons for attorney discipline are professional misconduct and criminal convictions (Krom 2019). Of particular note when it comes to disciplinary actions are Model Rules 1.1 Competence, 1.4 Communication, and 1.15 Client Funds which are prone to being violated more frequently (Johnstone 2004).

Attorneys may be referred to state disciplinary boards by clients, colleagues, supervisors, and/or judicial officers. Any number of situations may arise which could lead to a grievance with the state bar. When it comes to the more obvious effects of attorney mental illness on work product, clients may inevitably notice and report behavior indicative of negligence such as limited work being performed on the case, missed deadlines, adverse judgments, poor communication, or failures to appear (Klingen 2002). Aside from attorney negligence, cases handled by impaired attorneys may end up being referred to the state bar such as when judgment is entered based on the merits, when the attorney engages in malpractice, or due to the attorney's actions which are not provable as malpractice (Klingen 2002). Of course, clients are not obligated to file a grievance against their attorney but fellow attorneys may be required to do so.

For peer attorneys, filing a report with the state bar against another attorney can depend on the employment setting and the level of awareness regarding any past or current misconduct. Attorneys who work in midsize or large law firms, colleagues and/or supervisors may apprise the impaired attorney of any obvious deficits under Model Rule 8.3(a) Reporting Professional Misconduct. This rule, when combined with Model Rule 5.1 Responsibilities of a Partner of Supervisory Lawyer, requires the law firm to report the impaired attorney for discipline. If, however, the firm is able to successfully manage an impaired attorney without causing harm to any clients, they do not need to file a report. Law firms who have the resources can handle impaired attorneys on staff by offering supervision on cases, restricting the attorney's ability to handle matters, or preventing the attorney from even providing services during the period of impairment (Libby 2003). The law firm can also reassign an impaired attorney to less stressful responsibilities, such as swapping out a hostile takeover for drafting a transaction (Libby 2003).

WHO GETS DISCIPLINED

It has been said the larger the number of attorneys working at a particular law firm, the lower the rate of disciplinary actions (Hansen 2003). Given the distribution of attorney work and demographics, it may come as no surprise then that attorneys who work in small firms or are solo practitioners are referred to the state bar more often than other types of attorneys. The ABA Journal (Hansen 2003) reported, for example, that attorneys in California who worked in small firms or were solo made up 98 percent of the attorneys who were disciplined between 2000 and 2001. Inquiries by other states into who gets disciplined also revealed an imbalance with solo attorneys receiving more complaints and thus more sanctions (Hansen 2003). These results were further supported by a University of Nebraska-Lincoln study (Piquero et al. 2016) that found being a solo attorney increased the odds of having a complaint forwarded to the state bar grievance committee for consideration of discipline. In terms of gender and seniority, law professors Curtis and Kaufman (2004) found that in a Florida sample of disciplined attorneys male attorneys tended to be sanctioned more than female attorneys and that attorneys who practiced longer were more likely to be disciplined.

Additionally, inequities as to who gets sanctioned has further raised questions about racial disparity within the legal profession. Because a significant proportion of attorneys who identify as an ethnic minority tend to work in small firms or as solo practitioners, their likelihood of being disciplined increases.

Attorneys who happen to be licensed in more than one state may find themselves more at risk of being disciplined by multiple states. Most U.S. jurisdictions allow for reciprocal disciplinary actions against attorneys. Reciprocal actions between states occur when an attorney is licensed in multiple jurisdictions, such as two or more states, and after being disciplined by one jurisdiction, is then subject to discipline by the other. An example of this is an attorney who is licensed in both California and Nevada, gets disbarred in California and then is later disbarred in Nevada (after the Nevada disciplinary body reviews the California misconduct). It is important to note disciplinary boards and judges are not required to hand out the same consequences as other states, meaning discipline can be inconsistently meted out by jurisdictions.

DISCIPLINE PROCEDURES

Attorney discipline procedures function much like any other civil proceeding with notice, discovery, and a trial (New York State Bar 2015), however, some states take on a more criminal approach to discipline (Mogill 2014). Unless the complaint is dismissed, the disciplinary process will proceed. Attorneys who are unable to afford legal representation are not entitled to appointed counsel (Mogill 2014), and many disciplined attorneys end up representing themselves.

Disciplinary counsel, who acts as a prosecutor, evaluates and investigates the charges against the attorney and may prosecute, dismiss, stay, or petition the court. When a complaint against an attorney is referred for further review, a hearing committee comprised of two bar members and one public member carries out the hearing on the misconduct and presents its findings, conclusions, and recommendations to the disciplinary board (American Bar Association 2020f). Hearing committees conduct trials on formal charges where their decisions need not be unanimous. Hearing committee chairs may approve, reject, or modify any recommendations in addition to conducting prehearing conferences and deciding prehearing motions (American Bar Association 2020f). Once the hearing committee makes their recommendations, the attorney is free to stipulate to the proposed sanctions. Attorneys who do not agree with the hearing committee recommendations may challenge the decision, and a disciplinary board will then review and finalize sanctions, if applicable. Decisions by disciplinary boards are conclusive, meaning that appeal is not available to attorneys who wish to petition the sanctions (Mogill 2014).

Testimony

To request mitigation for a mental health or substance use condition, attorneys must introduce evidence of the impairment. Generally, this is accomplished through the attorney's own oral testimony but may be initiated via written testimony. Attorneys subject to discipline are allowed to present evidence of a mental health disorder or treatment by expert testimony just like any other litigant. The experts used for disciplinary proceedings are typically psychiatrists, psychologists, social workers, or any other licensed mental health professional involved in the diagnosis and treatment of mental health and/or substance use issues. As in any trial proceeding, testifying experts are vetted by the factfinder; in this case, the hearing judge or hearing panel.

Relying on expert testimony can present several challenges in attorney disciplinary proceedings. For one, any mental health provider treating the attorney may not be accepted as an expert but rather a personal witness who could testify as to the attorney's mental health treatment and observations during therapy.[7] Treating therapists may, among other reasons, not be available for court appearance due to work obligations or may feel uncomfortable offering testimony on behalf of their patient if they are unfamiliar with court proceedings. Expert witnesses, on the other hand, who could offer objective testimony as to their impressions of the attorney's mental health status may be more readily available as they would be hired to come to court, but added expenses during a time where many attorneys may be restricted from earning an income could be cost-prohibitive. Secondly, the factfinder may reject the expert's testimony altogether due to inadmissibility or worse, on the merits. In situations where the hearing panel or disciplinary board are simply not persuaded by the witness's testimony, the attorney may end up bereft of relief. Rejecting a sympathetic witness's testimony at a disciplinary hearing can be devastating for an attorney who is depending on the witness to validate the attorney's arguments.

MENTAL HEALTH AND SUBSTANCE USE RATES OF DISCIPLINARY ACTION

There appears to be a significant disparity in rates of disciplinary action when it comes to attorneys who endorse mental health and/or substance use problems vs. the overall population of disciplined attorneys. The South Carolina Office of Disciplinary Counsel, for example, reported that in the fiscal year 2018–2019 there were a total of 20 known disciplinary cases involving either mental health or substance use (South Carolina Judicial Department 2021). Of those 20 cases which involved 14 attorneys, five reported issues with alcohol, three reported illegal drugs, three reported Bipolar Disorder, two reported depression, one reported PTSD, and one reported an unknown mental health/substance use problem. Of these cases, 65 percent resulted in disciplinary action which, in comparison to South Carolina's overall discipline rate of 12.63 percent,[8] is a stunning difference. This means that attorneys who disclose having a problem with mental health or substance use are more than five times more likely to be disciplined than the general pool of disciplined attorneys.

Additionally, researchers have hypothesized that younger attorneys encounter disciplinary action earlier in their careers which may be due to mental health and/or substance use issues. In a study published in 2018, a researcher from Harvard University found that millennial attorneys (defined as those born between 1980–1992) were disciplined early on in their careers, typically within the first few years of practice (Edwards 2018). This finding raised issues of possible undetected or untreated mental health and/or substance use problems in young attorneys which may become exacerbated as the attorney's career progresses (Edwards 2018; Miranda 2018).

DISCIPLINE ALTERNATIVES

Under Model Rule 9(B) outlining Lesser Misconduct, alternatives to discipline may be considered for attorneys who have engaged in minor misconduct. Attorneys eligible for lesser misconduct charges may continue to practice law without any license restrictions. Alternatives to serious discipline include arbitration, mediation, lawyer assistance, psychological counseling, continuing education, ethics school, or other authorized alternatives (Model Rule 11(G). Courts should consider the following factors for attorneys who are eligible for alternatives: whether the discipline to be imposed would be no more severe than reprimand or admonition, whether the attorney could benefit from the program, the attorney's aggravating or mitigating factors, and whether diversion was previously attempted (Model Rule 11(G)(3).

NON-PUBLIC DISCIPLINARY ACTION

Non-public disciplinary action is used for minor violations that result in little to no injury to the client, the public, the legal system, or the profession (American Bar Association 2020f). These types of actions are non-public[9] and include letters of caution, letters of admonition, and private reproval.

Letter of Caution

A letter of caution[10] is an informational communication to an attorney advising of minor inappropriate behavior and any violations of ethical standards. Letters of caution often are educational and meant to serve as a warning of possible future disciplinary action if the attorney continues to engage in the behavior that initially led to the letter of caution. Some examples[11] of behavior that may prompt a letter of caution are:

- failing to return telephone calls
- neglecting to promptly advance a client's civil matters

- minor violations involving attorney trust accounts
- failing to provide retainer agreements
- entering into business transactions with clients
- receiving a DUI/DWI
- holding oneself out as a partnership when there is no partnership
- failing to specify whether an ad is attorney advertising
- misleading others to believe the attorney is a specialist in an area of law
- waiving a client's rights without their consent
- making malicious remarks or harassing comments towards opposing parties and/or government officials in and out of the courtroom
- filing a frivolous lawsuit
- failing to promptly return files
- failing to supervise non-attorney debt collectors which resulted in minor consumer law violations

Letter of Admonition

A letter of admonition is a written form of discipline requiring the hearing committee chair's approval and the attorney's consent (American Bar Association 2020f). It takes the letter of caution one step further and officially acknowledges that the attorney's conduct was improper, although it does not restrict the attorney's license or ability to practice law. A letter of admonition is generally non-public[12] and sometimes referred to as private reproval. Some examples of behavior that may prompt a letter of admonition are:

- Neglecting client matters which resulted in detriment to the client
- Violating attorney trust accounts
- Improperly notarizing affidavits
- Collecting excessive fees
- Sending a sarcastic letter to a judge
- Contacting opposing parties who are represented in a personal injury matter
- Engaging in transactions which improperly benefit the attorney when handling a client's wills and trust matters
- Violating confidentiality of a disciplinary investigation by disclosing information to a third-party

Some jurisdictions allow for private reprovals. This type of disciplinary action occurs when the attorney is found responsible for misconduct and is not suspended from practicing law. Because this action is private, there is generally no public disclosure made on the attorney's record.

PUBLIC DISCIPLINARY ACTIONS

In addition to court order or stipulation, courts may impose disciplinary actions such as admonition, reprimand, probation, suspension, and disbarment under Model Rule 10(A)(1). Public disciplinary actions are appropriate when an attorney has been reprimanded, placed on probation, suspended, or disbarred. These types of disciplinary action are the subject of this book in terms of data.

Public Reproval

Public reproval, or public reprimand, is imposed in cases involving minor misconduct and occurs after the hearing on the misconduct has taken place. In a public reproval/reprimand, the Disciplinary Board will serve the attorney in writing before publishing the notice (American Bar Association 2020f). Publicly reproved attorneys are found to be culpable of professional misconduct but still able to continue practicing without any interruption. Depending on any imposed requirements, the attorney may have to comply with additional probation standards such as retaking the state's ethics exam.

Probation

Probation is imposed when the attorney is able to work but still requires supervision (American Bar Association 2020f). Probation terms are generally not renewed and the ABA suggests that harsher discipline actions should be considered when the issues that gave rise to the probation are not resolved within the specified time period (American Bar Association 2020f).

Suspension

Attorneys who are suspended are typically ineligible to practice law for a defined period of time of no more than three years (American Bar Association 2020f). Suspended attorneys may be required to complete conditions of probation such as retaking the state ethics exam or submitting to random drug tests or daily remote monitoring. Suspension periods can vary and range from 90 days to multiple years, although Model Rule 10 recommends against indefinite suspensions, stating that suspensions should define a minimum time period for imposition. During suspension, the attorney is required to notify clients of their license status and may not perform legal work until they have been unsuspended.

DISBARMENT

Disbarment occurs when an attorney's license is revoked and they are removed from the roll of attorneys. Disbarment represents the most serious disciplinary action a state bar or state court can take against an attorney and has even been referred to as "'capital punishment' in the economic sense" for it cuts off an attorney's ability to work (Chinaris 2005, 870). Attorneys who are disbarred are ineligible to practice law and must notify their clients of their status. Disbarment standards vary; in New York, for example, the state carries an automatic or mandatory disbarment for any attorney convicted of a felony. Thus, convictions for felony drunk driving (Burge 2017), delivery of a controlled substance (*Matter of Smith* 2019), or tax evasion and making false statements (*Matter of Cohen* 2019) can, and have, resulted in disbarment.

Although disbarment generally represents a serious violation of the profession's standards, it does not always permanently preclude an attorney from returning to law. Depending on the circumstances and the curative efforts made by the disbarred attorney during the disbarment period, some attorneys may be eligible for readmission. Readmission restores an attorney's license to practice and is the only way a disbarred attorney can come back from dismissal.[13]

OTHER ACTIONS

Other actions the state bar disciplinary board may handle are resignations and reinstatements. In resignation, an attorney may choose to voluntarily resign (or surrender) while disciplinary charges are pending so as to avoid being disbarred. With reinstatement, a suspended attorney may petition the state bar to have their license returned after completing probation requirements and/ or waiting for the required time period following discipline (American Bar Association 2020e).

One uncommon action the board may take is a disability suspension. Despite its name, a disability suspension is not a disciplinary action; rather, it "serves as a door for impaired attorneys to exit the legal profession until they are successfully rehabilitated" (Heil 1993, 1293). A disability suspension can be triggered by an acute event, such as a psychiatric hospitalization, and places the attorney on inactive status so they are unable to practice law during the period of inactivity. This option appears relatively rare as only some states, including Ohio, Colorado, and Iowa, employ a disability suspension.

AGGRAVATING AND MITIGATING FACTORS

In general, most state bars have adopted the ABA's standards for aggravating and mitigating factors. State bars often weigh aggravating factors when determining the appropriate disciplinary action to take against an attorney. Aggravating factors, as the name implies, reduces the likelihood of getting off scot-free, and if the attorney is found to have several aggravating factors it is very likely the state court will impose a more serious form of discipline.

There are many kinds of aggravating factors. The list of aggravating factors[14] includes prior disciplinary offenses, dishonest or selfish motive, a pattern of misconduct, multiple offenses, bad faith, false statements or deceptive practices, refusal to acknowledge the wrongful nature of conduct, vulnerability of the victim, substantial experience in practicing law, and indifference to making restitution (American Bar Association 2020e). Disciplinary boards apply aggravating factors, based upon the attorney's misconduct itself and/or the attorney's misbehavior surrounding the disciplinary process, automatically.

Mitigating factors, on the other hand, can offset the aggravating factors presented and reduce or minimize the severity of discipline. Mitigating factors include an absence of prior disciplinary record, absence of dishonest or selfish motive, personal or emotional problems, good faith, remoteness of prior offenses, cooperation in proceedings, remorse, character or reputation, inexperience in practicing the law, physical or mental disability or impairment, delay in disciplinary proceedings, interim rehabilitation, and imposition of other penalties or sanctions.

The primary mitigating factors that pertain to mental health and/or substance use mitigation are physical or mental disability or impairment (this includes chemical dependency)[15] and personal or emotional problems. When state disciplinary boards determine appropriate sanctioning, they often weigh all of the factors of the attorney's circumstances before issuing a final sanction. States that follow the ABA's test under Standards for Imposing Lawyer Sanction 9.32(i) use the following four elements when evaluating an attorney for mitigation for mental disability or chemical dependency:

1. there is medical evidence that the respondent is affected by a chemical dependency or mental disability;
2. the chemical dependency or mental disability caused the misconduct;
3. the respondent's recovery from the chemical dependency or mental disability is demonstrated by a meaningful and sustained period of successful rehabilitation; and

4. the recovery arrested the misconduct and recurrence of that misconduct is unlikely (American Bar Association 1992, 18).

Despite there being only four elements[16] to prove, the mitigation standard for mental disability or chemical dependency carries a significant burden. In fact, the guidelines for mitigation have been criticized for acting as "obstacle[s]" rather than advantages for attorneys given how difficult it can be for attorneys to receive mitigation (Rush 2011, 942). The ABA, for its part, does not offer much direction for evaluators when it comes to weighing factors either so much discretion is left up to each disciplinary board to decide what and how factors are weighed (Luty 2004).

The ABA also does not explicitly state which impairments qualify for mitigation, although it appears from brief case law reviews that many of the impairments which qualify for mitigation are recognized disorders that can be diagnosed using the DSM-5 (Commission on Lawyer Assistance Programs 2020a). It is up to individual state disciplinary boards to determine whether an attorney's mental impairment counts towards mitigation. In the past, the ABA has published case law reviews showing that attorneys have received mitigation for various conditions including alcohol dependence, prescription painkiller addiction, gambling, and depression (Commission on Lawyer Assistance Programs 2020a). In recent years, some courts have stated compassion fatigue may count as a mitigating factor (Bahn 2019; Rubin 2018) but "sex addiction" does not (Rubin 2015).

CRITICISMS OF MODERN ATTORNEY DISCIPLINE PRACTICES

Given that most disciplinary actions that are initiated are never made public, it is difficult to accurately get a true understanding of how the attorney disciplinary process works. While the burden of proof in disciplinary hearings is usually clear and convincing evidence, for instance, this is not systematically applied and court opinions on disciplinary cases have been criticized as being "inconsistent" (Gillers 2014, 486), lacking in uniformity (Fabian and Reinthaler 2001), and "secret" (Levin 2007, 2), making studying trends in cases difficult. Further, private actions that the state bar may take against an attorney are withheld from the public. The types of cases, unique factors, and personal details of the attorneys themselves are a mystery to anyone who investigates these matters.[17] Similarly, there are questions about the fairness of who receives discipline with respect to race and diversity issues (State Bar of California 2019). As such, some opponents to privacy have argued for more transparency in the disciplinary process, citing possible First

Amendment right of access claims (Levin 2007). To date, however, none of the state bars provide information about closed or dismissed cases, and some state bars provide no information at all on any disciplinary cases unless specifically requested in writing. The confidentiality surrounding attorney discipline may thus be seen as a hindrance to studying the cases that are referred to state bars.

Another issue is that disciplining attorneys to protect the public creates a false narrative that an actively practicing attorney is safe and an inactive attorney is unsafe. Attorneys who are privately disciplined, such as in reproval or censure, may continue accepting new clients and working on cases even while currently being disciplined for violations (Gillers 2014). Likewise, attorneys who have been suspended or disbarred may have resolved the issues that first led to their discipline and actually be perfectly capable of resuming their work duties.

Critics have also argued disciplining a disabled attorney contravenes the Americans with Disabilities Act (ADA) of 1990.[18] The law does not provide disciplinary immunity for attorneys with disabilities who engage in misconduct; rather, the ADA was meant to safeguard individuals with disabilities, including attorneys, against discrimination (Kratovil 2000). However, as Kratovil (2000) pointed out, state bars "continued to believe that these disabled attorneys deserved discipline—just less of it" (998). Consequently some attorneys subjected to discipline have unsuccessfully appealed their cases under the ADA on the basis of mental health and/or substance use disorders.[19] Courts handling these cases have pointed to the overarching goal ("to protect the public from harm") of most state's disciplinary boards before dismissing attorney appeals.

BACKGROUND OF OUR RESEARCH

We began exploring attorney mental health and substance use problems by analyzing published disciplinary opinions of individuals who were reprimanded, suspended, or disbarred by U.S. state and territory licensing authorities. We examined clinical diagnoses, symptoms, functional impairments, and treatment presented through the attorney's own testimony or by expert and other witness testimony during disciplinary hearings and compared the clinical information to factors germane to attorney discipline such as outcome of the case, type of sanction, persuasiveness of testimony, and mitigation efforts.

To collect quantitative and qualitative data, we utilized legal search engine LexisNexis along with state bar records available to the public through bar association websites and state bar organization compilations such as annual reports. Using the most prevalent mental illness conditions found in attorney mental health literature and the more prevalent substances used by attorneys within the past 12 months (Krill et al. 2016), we searched for the following terms in attorney disciplinary proceedings: depression, anxiety, PTSD, bipolar disorder, alcohol, sedatives, opioids, stimulants, and cocaine.

We expected this research to contribute to current literature on attorney mental health by offering insights into an unseen segment of life. We endeavored to collect quantitative data and qualitative data and compare prevalence rates of mental health and substance use issues to previous research on attorneys under the assumption that attorneys would reveal significant mental health problems if their careers depended on it.

To provide a sense of how vast attorney discipline records are, for instance, our search of the 50 U.S. states and its territories using a 10-year date range from 2010 to 2020 revealed over 35,000 cases.[20] We further narrowed our search to include only reported cases which resulted in a sample of 9,942 cases. We found the term "stress" was included in approximately 2,500 cases; "depression" was named in almost 1,500 cases; "anxiety" in around 1,300 cases; "PTSD" in 550 cases; and "bipolar" in over 400 cases. For substances, alcohol was by far mentioned the most at over 400 cases followed by cocaine and stimulants. In the following chapters, we highlight the more salient cases found in research involving the previously mentioned diagnosable conditions.[21]

NOTES

1. In ascending order of severity these sanctions included: probation, admonition, reprimand, interim suspension, suspension, and disbarment (Kratovil 2000).

2. The ABA later published in 1994 the Model Rules for Judicial Disciplinary Enforcement for judges or judicial officers.

3. This figure does not include data from Connecticut, Mississippi, New York's 3rd Department, South Dakota, and West Virginia.

4. This figure does not include California.

5. In Nevada and Kentucky, disbarment is permanent with no possibility of reinstatement (Hudson 2020). Additionally, Louisiana can impose permanent disbarment on attorneys.

6. When compared to physicians and CPAs, attorneys were more likely to lose their license to practice, with disbarment, suspension, or surrender occurring in 76.8 percent of disciplinary actions (Krom 2019). Attorneys are disciplined on average about nine times more than CPAs and punished more severely than either physicians or CPAs (Krom 2019).

7. Treating therapist testimony is helpful and accepted, but we raise the issue of this testimony not being qualified as an expert witness because some hearing committees,

such as those in Washington state, require expert testimony to prove medical facts (Disciplinary Proceeding against Petersen 1993).

8. This figure represents the disciplined percentage of all South Carolina's attorneys.

9. In Arizona and Oregon, there are no private or non-public sanctions.

10. Depending on the jurisdiction, this may also be referred to as a letter of warning or letter of advisement.

11. These examples do not include all possible outcomes.

12. In Missouri, letters of admonition are public.

13. Some disbarred attorneys may choose to work as paralegals or perform other legal assistant-type work under the oversight of a licensed attorney. This is not the same as reinstatement, however, because a disbarred attorney cannot perform the same services as a licensed attorney, e.g., offering legal advice.

14. Some states use "mental state" as an aggravating factor against the attorney which is not to be confused with mitigation for mental health or substance use. Mental state is typically answered using the following questions: "Did the lawyer act intentionally, knowingly, or negligently?" (American Bar Association 1992, 4). An intentional mental state warrants the highest responsibility for misconduct. In our research, when disciplinary boards find an attorney intentionally engaged in misconduct, the board typically uses mental state as an aggravating factor.

15. Disciplinary boards and state bar courts "have never recognized alcoholism and/or substance abuse as a defense to professional misconduct," although it may be used as a mitigating factor (Rovzar 2015, 448).

16. Some states require fewer elements.

17. Before 2015 the Vermont State Bar made disciplinary case records anonymous.

18. The ADA (1990) states in pertinent part: ". . . no qualified individual with a disability shall, by reason of such disability, be excluded from participation in or be denied the benefits of the services, programs, or activities of a public entity, or be subjected to discrimination by any such entity." It is of note that the ADA (1990) excludes current drug users from protection but does apply to individuals with a past history of drug use.

19. See Columbus Bar Ass'n v. Elsass, 86 Ohio St. 3d 195 (1999) where the court rejected the attorney's claim of an ADA violation for his drug addiction and Florida Bar v. Clement, 662 So.2d 690 (1995) where the court denied the attorney relief under the ADA and disbarred him despite his diagnosis of bipolar disorder.

20. This number is an estimate of the total number of attorney disciplinary cases published in the US between 2010–2020. Duplicates, errors, or other unforeseen issues with estimating cases may result in an over- or underestimate of the true number.

21. The cases presented in the following chapters do not recount every detail contained within the court decisions. Some facts may be omitted for purposes of brevity.

Chapter 4

Mental Illness in the Legal Profession

Sadly, and rather expectedly as we have discussed in previous chapters, the workloads, high expectations, and minimal support offered in the work environment often leads to or exacerbates significant mental health problems for attorneys. Because attorneys can manifest a variety of mental health issues and disorders that may go undetected by others, even by the attorneys themselves, we explored and analyzed state disciplinary proceedings in search of respondents who introduced evidence of a mental health condition.

DEPRESSION

One of the most commonly reported mental health disorders in attorneys is depression (Krill et al. 2016). Depression is characterized by sad, irritable, or low mood along with functional impairment. The disorder is broad; it can range from mild to severe and can last for years or weeks depending on the person. Individuals who are depressed have more difficulty experiencing positive feelings and may lose interest in activities they once enjoyed. Overall, depression can significantly affect the way a person thinks, feels, and behaves which can result in deleterious consequences for attorneys.

Depression can be diagnosed under various names as there are eight depressive disorders listed in the DSM-5, but typically Major Depressive Disorder is the standard diagnosis. According to the American Psychiatric Association (2013), the primary criteria for Major Depressive Disorder is:

- Feeling sad or having a depressed mood
- Loss of interest or pleasure in activities once enjoyed
- Changes in appetite—weight loss or gain unrelated to dieting
- Trouble sleeping or sleeping too much

- Loss of energy or increased fatigue
- Increase in purposeless physical activity or slowed movements or speech
- Feeling worthless or guilty
- Difficulty thinking, concentrating, or making decisions
- Thoughts of death or suicide

While depressive episodes can resolve on their own within weeks, the more severe cases can last much longer and be debilitating. Regardless of severity and duration, depression can wreak havoc on an attorney's personal life and work commitments. Court deadlines may be easily forgotten or not seem so important to a depressed attorney. Workloads, too, may feel insurmountable when faced with the overwhelming despair of depression.

Our examination of depression in attorney disciplinary cases revealed some unexpected findings. First, we found a total of 260 court opinions where an attorney presented with depression which represented only 2.4 percent of the cases, a small fraction when compared to overall prevalence rates in community and attorney samples.

Table 4.1 *Comparison of mental health and substance use disorder prevalence rates in U.S. attorney disciplinary cases, 2010–2020*

Mental Health or Substance-Related and Addictive Disorder	Annual prevalence rate in U.S. adults[1]	Prevalence rate in attorneys[2]	Prevalence rate in disciplinary cases
Alcohol	*8.5 percent*	*20.6 percent*	*2.2 percent*
Anxiety	*-*	*61.1 percent*	*0.7 percent*
• *Panic Disorder*	*2.0-3.0 percent*	*8.0 percent*	*-*
• *Generalized Anxiety Disorder*	*7.0 percent*	*-*	*-*
Bipolar Disorder	*1.0-2.0 percent*	*2.4 percent*	*0.3 percent*
Depression	*7.0 percent*	*45.7 percent*	*2.4 percent*
PTSD	*3.5 percent*	*-*	*0.3 percent*
Opioids	*0.37 percent*	*5.6 percent*	*0.1 percent*
Sedatives	*0.2 percent*	*15.7 percent*	*0.2 percent*
Stimulants	*0.2-0.3 percent*	*4.8 percent*	*0.2 percent*

1 American Psychiatric Association (2013).
2 Krill et al. (2016).

Depression was the most common condition we discovered, reflecting more than a third of the cases. In the following case examples, we describe several attorneys who reported that the effects of depression impacted their conduct.

CASE EXAMPLE #1: *DISCIPLINARY BOARD V. SUMMERS* (2012)

In September 2010, a client hired licensed North Dakota attorney Summers to modify a child support order. After mailing an $850 check to her office and not receiving a reply, the client emailed the law office to ask about the case. The client received no response. He emailed four more times before calling and leaving a voicemail message in November 2010. He did not receive a response to any of his emails or phone call. The day after he left the voice-mail, the client threatened to file a complaint with the State Bar Association of North Dakota against Summers if she did not respond to his inquiries. He again received no response. The client then contacted the state bar and filed a complaint against her. Soon afterwards, Summers emailed the client with attachments of work she had performed on the case. The client, however, could only view one of the attachments and that attachment needed to be corrected. He asked her several questions including how much of the retainer remained, how long it would take for her to make the changes he requested, and whether she needed anything else from him. Summers replied that she would refund the client his $850 retainer if he no longer wished to pursue the modification order. The client confirmed he did not wish to go ahead with the order, and Summers refunded him his $850.

In response to the client's complaint, the State Bar Association of North Dakota charged Summers with two violations under North Dakota's Rules for Professional Conduct (NDRPC). The hearing committee alleged she violated NDRPC 1.3 Diligence that states "a lawyer shall act with reasonable diligence and promptness in representing a client." They also found she violated two sections of NDRPC 1.4(a) Communication under subsection (3) that states "a lawyer shall make reasonable efforts to keep the client reasonably informed about the status of a matter," and subsection (4) that states "a lawyer shall promptly comply with the client's reasonable requests for information."

At her hearing, Summers testified she had been suffering from depression throughout her representation of the client. Although there was no indication of when her depression began, she reported feeling depressed during her previous admonitions in 2009 and 2010 and that her condition had worsened upon finding out one of her employees had embezzled from her law office. She presented treatment records to the hearing panel detailing her history of depression. The panel noted her records indicated she had been evaluated for recurrent Major Depressive Disorder along with "dysthymia and anxiety disorder not otherwise specified" (*Summers* 2012, 368). Disciplinary counsel argued that Summers should not receive mitigation for her mental health issues because she failed to present expert testimony connecting her depression to her professional misconduct. The hearing panel, however, con-cluded she had shown the court that even without expert testimony her mental health issues were related to her behavior and considered this in mitigation. Summers' suspension of six months and one day was stayed for one year.

OUR VIEW

This case demonstrates how depression in attorneys can manifest. Diligence and communication, both ethical duties owed to clients, may be difficult to maintain during a depressed episode and may continue for quite some time if the attorney is experiencing a chronic depression such as dysthymia or major depression with comorbid dysthymia (commonly referred to as "double depression"). It appears here that Summers experienced recurrent episodes of major depression alongside dysthymia. She reported being depressed during previous disciplinary admonitions that occurred a year earlier which provides a clue as to the chronicity of her mental health issues. It also appears there was some type of a compounding effect on her depression given her report of experiencing worsening symptoms after finding out an employee embezzled from the firm.

Because depression is a disorder characterized by a lack of energy and turning away from once enjoyable activities, withdrawal and retreat into oneself is prominent. Contact—even with paying clients—can be a struggle resulting in poor communication and grievances. In this example, it appears Summers only got in contact with the client after he had reported her to the state bar disciplinary board. Clearly, waiting until a client files a report with the bar to communicate with them about their case is unacceptable but also understandable through the lens of chronic depression. Many individuals living with depression find getting out of bed challenging in itself; likewise, attorneys with depression may find returning a phone call or emailing a demand letter exhausting.[1]

Moreover, depression commonly involves an inability to maintain concen-tration or focus, making it much more difficult to perform tasks that were once effortless. It is unknown what the chain of events were leading up to Summers emailing the client the unsatisfactory attachments mentioned; but, it is clear that when she did return work product to him, some of the attach-ments were faulty (unable to be opened) and the only document the client could open needed correction. It is possible that symptoms of depression played a role in her ability to perform work including being able to concen-trate on emails and documents sent to the client. If at the time she had expe-rienced poor concentration and lack of focus, we would expect to see a lack of conscientiousness in her work product.

It is also worth mentioning that the hearing panel accepted written testimony regarding her mental health status in the form of treatment records. Not every hearing committee accepts testimony in this format; in fact, many of the cases we will discuss require a live expert to testify in the flesh. Differences in how evidence is presented and accepted demonstrate how inconsistently disciplinary boards apply mitigation standards.

CASE EXAMPLE #2: *DISCIPLINARY COUNSEL V. KARP* (2018)

The client, a Bulgarian ballroom dancer, wanted to transfer her non-immigration worker visa from the New Jersey dance studio she currently worked at to a new studio out in California. Karp informed the client he would be able to complete the petition to transfer her visa. She wired him a total of $1,075 for his anticipated work on the case including the filing fee. About seven months after he had initially told the client he had filed the petition, Karp submitted the paperwork to the government. He had signed the new dance studio employer's name on the petition, believing he had the authority to do so, and he made amends to a request for modification on the petition without consulting the client or the California studio. The transfer petition was ultimately denied. The client reported Karp to the Ohio Board of Professional Conduct, and the board charged him with violating several ethical rules related to his work on the client's visa. In addition to the misconduct on the case, the board alleged that Karp had used money in his client's trust account to pay for personal and business-related matters. Though he had another account, Karp explained to the board that as a solo attorney he preferred to take care of his expenses using one account instead of transferring funds between accounts. The board stipulated to a two-year suspension for Karp's misconduct, but the attorney objected and requested that his suspension be stayed in light of his mitigating factors.

Upon review of his case, the board discussed multiple aggravating[2] and mitigating[3] factors, one of which was Karp's mental disorder. To determine whether Karp's mental disorder constituted a mitigating factor, the board applied a four element test under Government of the Bar of Ohio Rule V(13(C)(7).[4] At his hearing, Karp's board-certified psychiatrist stated that the attorney had been diagnosed with Major Depressive Disorder and an "exacerbating" hypothyroidism, both conditions which he opined contributed to his misconduct. Karp indicated that a precipitating factor to his depression was a malpractice action against him where he, as in this case, had also failed to timely file a petition. He started taking medication and participating in psychotherapy in March and June of 2017, respectively. His psychiatrist reported

Karp was in compliance with his treatment and that as of two weeks before his disciplinary hearing his:

> . . .depression was essentially in remission; although I use that term a bit cautiously because under DSM to be classified as being in remission you need two months of not meeting criteria for major depression. So he was right at that line of two months. Close to it. But he was no longer feeling depressed. As I mentioned early [sic], his concentration was better, energy was better, sleep pattern was better. He was continuing to lose weight, which was a very positive thing. So again, fairly substantial improvement between September and November. (830)

Taking into consideration the psychiatrist's testimony, the Board declined to offer Karp full mitigation for his mental disorder because they were unclear as to whether he had achieved a "sustained period of successful treatment" as specified under Ohio rules. Thus, the Board rejected mitigation for his mental disorder and accepted the Disciplinary Board's recommendation to suspend Karp for two years.

OUR VIEW

In this case it appears the board wanted to see a period of time where Karp could demonstrate stability without any signs of impairment or dysfunction due to depression. His psychiatrist's testimony gave the impression the attorney was not out of the woods yet; he was described as "essentially in remission" and "right at that line," both phrases which at least in terms of the law do not indicate a definitive "yes" as to the question of whether the attorney can show a sustained period of treatment. It is unfortunate that the hearing in which the psychiatrist testified was not held one or two weeks later; the additional time could have made a difference with respect to the psychiatrist's testimony and in turn the Board's decision on whether to allow mitigation.

CASE EXAMPLE # 3: *IOWA V. MARKS* (2013)

An attorney who had previously been offered mitigation by the Iowa Attorney Disciplinary Board was told that his diagnosis of depression was now considered an aggravating factor. In 2009, Marks testified in his third disciplinary case that he admitted to overlooking two probate matters and explained that his misconduct was in part due to his mental health issues. He reported, at the time, having been diagnosed with depression in 2008 and was being treated with psychotropic medication and attending counseling. The board found that his mental health disorder was a mitigating factor before offering a "stern warning." The board stated:

> [Mr. Marks] is teetering on the brink of disaster. Although he is fit to practice law, he has fallen into a pattern of neglect and non-cooperation these past few years. If he does not remedy this behavior, he will receive a harsher sanction next time he appears before us. . . . Although we are sympathetic to the struggles Marks has endured with depression, his past conduct and record as a whole indicates he lacks diligence and professionalism. (*Marks* 2013, 201)

In 2013 when Marks was referred to the board again for four ethical violations (e.g., competence, diligence, expeditious litigation, misconduct), his mental health issues were unwelcomed. The board stated his depression "complicat[ed]" his current case; apparently, the board found the mismatch between his 2009 and 2013 treatment plan confusing. Whereas he seemed to be benefiting from a combination of medication and counseling in his 2009 case, here he reported managing his depressive symptoms through medication alone. Regarding any plans on returning to in-person therapy sessions, Marks acknowledged he "could probably benefit from more" and described counseling as "very helpful." He affirmed to the board that he had health insurance which could cover some therapy sessions. In a perplexing move, the board chose to "consider [Marks'] untreated chronic depression to be an aggravating factor" despite his testimony that he was treating his symptoms through medication. The board subsequently suspended him for a 90-day period and requested he undergo a fitness-for-duty evaluation upon reinstatement.

OUR VIEW

In this case it appears that the board would have benefited from education about the different treatments and therapies that are efficacious for depression. Psychotropic medication is often prescribed in conjunction with talk therapy but not always. Some individuals may find one or both helpful. Further, treatment plans change as do patient resources. It seems the board presumed that he should have continued with the same treatment he was prescribed in 2009. Although he had previously attended therapy sessions and confirmed he currently had insurance, it is unknown what barriers to attending counseling existed for him. Many patients struggle to find affordable counseling or therapists who take their insurance. Some patients with more chronic depression, such as Marks, may find it difficult to afford long-term therapy when their insurance runs out. Still, other factors such as availability of treatment providers within a particular geographic area can also affect patients. In any event, it is discouraging to see a Disciplinary Board penalize an attorney who is currently receiving mental health treatment.

CASE EXAMPLE #4: *LAWYER DISCIPLINARY BOARD V. THORN* (2016)

Solo practitioner Thorn was brought before the West Virginia Lawyer Disciplinary Board to address 11 complaints including one from another attorney. One of the complaints involved a client who had hired Thorn to represent her in a divorce proceeding. Thorn estimated he worked more than 14 hours on the case before the client requested to terminate him for not returning her phone calls and emails. Thorn acknowledged his communication failures and testified that "[b]ecause he suffered a period of depression during this time, he. . . was unable to muster the energy to hand-hold such clients." In a second case where Thorn was hired to represent a client on a habeas petition, the client complained that the attorney did not turn over their file to their new attorney in a timely manner. In response, Thorn stated that his "depression could have affected his ability to copy and turn over files."

At his hearing, Thorn offered testimony regarding his mental health. He reported experiencing a "deep and significant depression" from 2012–2013 after going through a divorce. He was so depressed he thought about "giving up, walking away, and surrendering his law license." He admitted to not being "professionally fit" to practice law while he was depressed due to his symptoms. An expert witness who reviewed Thorn's mental health history and met with him for two hours testified at the hearing that the attorney appeared to meet several criteria of depression because he had lost a significant amount of weight and experienced "hopelessness, worthlessness, and lack of ability to enjoy life for over a year." The witness added, "Mr. Thorn stayed home and avoided interaction with others much of the time." Additionally, the expert witness mentioned that Thorn revealed having thoughts of suicide during this period of time. Despite the severity of the nature of his depression, Thorn testified his depression had resolved on its own without any need for professional treatment and that he had taken steps to restore his practice.

Because he had not been seen by a mental health professional for treatment, Thorn had no medical records to submit to the court indicating diagnostic or treatment considerations. The board appeared somewhat unsure of how to weigh the evidence; it stated the expert witness did not distinguish whether Thorn's depression was "situational" or "clinical" and it noted that some of the client complaints fell outside of his reported span of depression. The board also expressed concern that Thorn had not immediately sought professional help or shared any back-up plans with the board in case a mental health crisis were to occur again. Accordingly, the board assigned less than the greatest weight of mitigation for Thorn's mental illness before suspending him for one year.

OUR VIEW

This case is in stark contrast to Case Example #1 where the respondent presented a detailed history of depression; in that case the documentation was helpful. Here, it appears through the attorney's own testimony and the social worker's evaluation that Thorn had experienced a period of depression. Thorn estimated his symptoms which included depressed mood, hopelessness, worthlessness, anhedonia, social isolation, significant weight loss, and suicidal ideation occurred over the course of a year or two following his divorce. Though evidence of his depression symptoms were presented in the hearing, the social worker who testified as an expert in the case did not offer a clear diagnosis to the board. To be fair, the social worker may not have been able to discern in the limited time he had with Thorn whether the attorney met criteria for depression. It is unfortunate that Thorn did not have a treating mental health clinician to testify or submit records on his behalf as to his diagnosis or treatment since it appears the court was looking for more definitive proof of his mental health condition at the time of his misconduct.

CASE EXAMPLE # 5: *IOWA V. BARRY* (2018)

In Iowa, an attorney's untreated depression was viewed as a mitigating factor. At the time of his disciplinary case, Barry was a partner at his law firm and was hired by the client to represent her in a divorce proceeding. In providing updates to the client and her family members, Barry misrepresented that he had filed the client's dissolution paperwork and showed them a fake divorce decree he had altered to appear genuine. A complaint against Barry was subsequently filed with the Iowa Attorney Disciplinary Board for the alleged fraud.

In mitigation, Barry submitted a letter to the hearing panel detailing his experience of "debilitating" depression during the time of this dissolution case. In the letter, he reported working for several years without receiving any mental health treatment—a fact the board stated was "an important mitigating factor" as well as one they expressed concern over. Barry had gone to about seven "counseling sessions" with a teacher at a yoga center and eight "one-day healing intensive[s]" which the board noted did not count towards mental health treatment because they were not facilitated by a licensed mental health professional. Barry did, however, relate that he anticipated attending a residential rehabilitation center in California. Barry's letter went on to connect his depression to his misconduct: he stated the depression he experienced inhibited him from submitting his work since he "just became paralyzed and couldn't do it." The board noted that Barry's letter appeared to account for the problems with diligence on the case but did not clarify questions surrounding his false statements made to the client or her family about the paperwork. After considering all of the evidence he presented, the board only allowed for minor mitigation on Barry's depression.

OUR VIEW

In this case, it appeared the attorney had been struggling to work despite suffering from chronic untreated symptoms of depression. Regrettably he worked for several years without addressing his mental health needs, and when he finally did seek treatment the board did not credit his sessions due to his provider being a non-mental health professional. This shows it is important for attorneys seeking mitigation to (1) seek help; and (2) ensure that the provider is a licensed mental health counselor or other approved provider that the court will credit for purposes of receiving mental health treatment.

Second, it appears the attorney needed to do a more complete job of linking his misconduct to his reported mental disorder. In the court's view, this would include indicating how his depression was linked to his misrepresentations to his clients. Though Barry was able to tie in his depression to his lack of diligence on the case, he failed to connect his symptoms to his false statements. It would therefore behoove attorneys seeking mitigation to sufficiently address questions regarding the mental health/misconduct nexus.

CASE EXAMPLE # 6: *NEBRASKA V. PERSON* (2018)

Person, a probate attorney with more than 48 years of experience from Nebraska, argued in his 2018 trial for ethical violations that he had suffered from depression during the time of his misconduct. Person's misconduct included failing to respond to orders to show cause, failing to appear at a hearing, and misrepresenting to the court that he had filed a tax form with the IRS when he had not. He reported experiencing depression after a "severe motor vehicle accident, the loss of his father in 2007, and his brother's retiring from the practice of law" (*Person* 2018, 862). The Nebraska Supreme Court noted Person began his legal career practicing law alongside his father in 1970, and it appears his father and his brother supported his legal career up until the latter part of the 2000s when the attorney's family members either passed away or retired. He reported feeling "overburdened" following his father's death and brother's retirement but was not aware of his mental health issues during this period (*Person* 2018, 862).

The court was unconvinced, however, and stated: "[T]he record contains no medical evidence that the injuries [the attorney] received in his accident were direct and substantial contributing factors for his conduct. As such, the referee discounted those claims" (*Person* 2018, 862). In a further blow, the court added that the attorney's isolation during his time of depression should be viewed critically when they said, "Moreover, [his] lack of a support system in which to seek professional assistance and counsel with regard to decision-making [sic] is a cause for concern. This need for support, and accompanying lack of support, lead to the unavoidable concern for the protection of the public" (*Person* 2018, 862).

Although the court recognized some factors which were in favor of the attorney,[5] they ultimately suspended him for a minimum of two years, after which he would be eligible to apply for reinstatement.

OUR VIEW

Based on the reasoning presented in this case, it appears the court completely ignored Person's statement regarding depression. The court only mentions a lack of "medical evidence" in his record with no mention of any absence of mental health evidence. In fact, the term "depression" only appears once in the court order in the paragraph where the court summarizes Person's report as to what led to the disciplinary complaint. It is possible that without further evidence in the form of expert testimony or submission of treatment records, the court would have reached the same conclusion as to Person's ability to practice but it is nonetheless surprising that the court failed to address his report of experiencing depression given that he had suffered a major car accident, was apparently still grieving over the loss of his father, and no longer had his brother's support at their firm.

This case highlights that some courts may ignore testimony from the complainant (attorney) regarding mental health issues and may even be biased towards evidence of physical or medical injuries vs. mental health issues. This harkens back to a time in the law when emotional distress claims had to be physically tangible. Of course, we know today that "[s]evere emotional damages can occur in the absence of any physical injury" but the idea that there is a separation between physical and emotional harm may persist (Bornstein 2009). Bornstein (2009) says this is troublesome for two reasons:

(1) emotional suffering can take just as long to heal from as physical injury; and (2) the mind-body connection plays a pivotal role in overall health. Here, it is unclear whether the court implied a bias towards physical injury but this case does show that testimony regarding a serious mental health condition can be dismissed.

BIPOLAR DISORDER

Similar to depression, Bipolar Disorder is another mental illness involving mood episodes. You may have heard Bipolar Disorder previously referred to as "manic depression" because of the distinct, intense mood episodes associated with the illness. Bipolar disorder is thought of as a brain disorder that can cause significant disruption to a person's thoughts, feelings, and behaviors. When experiencing a manic episode, the individual with Bipolar Disorder may act in an uncharacteristic, abnormal way from their typical presentation (American Psychiatric Association 2013). The combination of manic symptoms can be particularly dangerous, leading to reckless behaviors that are "likely to have catastrophic consequences" (American Psychiatric Association 2013, 129).

Bipolar disorder is categorized into three types: Bipolar I Disorder, Bipolar II Disorder, and Cyclothymic Disorder. Bipolar I Disorder is known for more significant manic episodes and typically requires psychiatric hospitalizations during acute phases of the illness. The estimated prevalence in the U.S. for Bipolar Disorder I is 0.6 percent (American Psychiatric Association 2013; Merikangas et al. 2007). Bipolar II Disorder is characterized by states of hypomania and individuals may spend more time managing depressive symptoms during low periods. Depression may be present in either illness but not necessarily, and both typically require medication management throughout the individual's lifetime to control the effects of the disorder. Cyclothymic Disorder is a milder version than either Bipolar I or II where individuals experience frequent mood swings over a period of at least two years.

As stated, bipolar disorder includes both symptoms of depression and mania. Mania is diagnosed when the individual experiences several changes in behavior such as:

- Decreased need for sleep
- Increased or faster speech
- Uncontrollable racing thoughts or ideas
- Distractibility
- Increased activity
- Increased risky behavior

Despite bipolar disorder being known for alternating intense moods of mania or depression, people living with the illness are just like non-bipolar people in that they also experience other moods and may be quite neutral for periods of time. During these well-adjusted periods, individuals may resume normal levels of functioning without issue.

Any attorney aware of and managing a bipolar disorder should be aware of their mental health needs and hopefully taking their medications as prescribed. If an attorney were to experience a manic episode during their career, it could be destructive given the impulsive and reckless behaviors that can accompany a bipolar diagnosis. The following case example shows what may happen to an attorney with bipolar disorder.

CASE EXAMPLE #7: *IOWA V. KINGERY* (2015)

Solo practitioner and court-appointed counsel Kingery was reported to the Disciplinary Board for alleged violations she committed in four matters. In the first matter, Kingery represented a defendant on his criminal appeal. She performed some work on the case by filing a certificate and ordering a transcript; however, it was noted that she failed to file a brief. Consequently, the clerk submitted a notice of default judgment on July 30, 2013, informing the attorney that she needed to submit the missing paperwork before the deadline. Kingery did not file the paperwork. Two months later the court appointed new counsel and sua sponte filed a complaint with the Board. In the second matter, Kingery was hired to represent a client in a divorce proceeding. The attorney filed an application for rule to show cause and met with the client to prepare responses on discovery requests but did not respond to the client's requests for status updates from July to September 2013. During that time, Kingery had missed a discovery response deadline. The client fired Kingery from the case and reported her complaint to the board. In the third matter, a district court judge who became aware of Kingery's conduct while she performed court-appointed work also filed a complaint with the Board. Kingery failed to appear for her clients' arraignments, did not return phone calls, and was removed from representing several clients in 2013. In two cases, neither Kingery nor the defendant-clients appeared in court; the judge issued bench warrants, arrested the clients, and sent them to jail for the nonappearance. District attorneys and judicial officers "noted Kingery's absence from the courthouse as it stretched over several months." In the fourth case, a client hired Kingery in February 2013 to draft a property deed. He grew "impatient" after waiting several months for the work to be completed, and when Kingery handed the deed over to the client in September 2013, he noted there were errors and corrections that needed to be made. Kingery, however, did not make corrections to the deed or even reply to the client's messages, so he terminated the relationship before filing his complaint with the board. In all four instances, the board found that she had violated several ethics rules including neglect, attorney-client communication, unreasonable expenses, mandatory withdrawal, failing to expedite litigation, duty to avoid making false statements, and conduct prejudicial to the administration of justice.

In mitigation, Kingery testified she had initially been diagnosed with bipolar disorder while in law school and that she takes psychotropic medication to manage her symptoms. In 2013, the same year as contained in the four separate complaints, she married a non-U.S. citizen who lived in Europe and she reported that their primary mode of communication is via phone or video chat. She noted that her relationship with her husband has caused her much stress due to the immigration barriers that prevented him from coming to the U.S. to live with her. During this period of time after her wedding (2013) she began drinking more frequently and in higher quantities. She "spun out of control." Her regular daily schedule at the time involved "buying alcohol, drinking alcohol, and sleeping." She stated she stopped communicating altogether with clients, judges, opposing counsel, and the board. In early 2014 Kingery reported seeking treatment for her mental health and substance use issues. She completed a detox program, attended inpatient treatment and outpatient treatment. She began attending weekly support groups, church functions, and the state's lawyer assistance program. The board afforded her mitigation for her mental health disorder before suspending her license indefinitely.

OUR VIEW

Even though the attorney sought and received comprehensive treatment for her mental health and substance use issues, the board suspended her license. This is highly discouraging—Kingery clearly suffered from a severe mental health disorder for which she was receiving treatment. Perhaps expert testimony would have been helpful in this case to further emphasize Kingery's issues and follow-up treatment. Regardless, this case offers an example of the perspective some state disciplinary boards may take when it comes to handling an attorney's serious mental illness.

CASE EXAMPLE #8: *FLORIDA V. LITTLE* (2018)

Little, a Foley & Lardner, LLP, law firm partner out of Florida, accessed private client information through his firm's database. He and a colleague he tipped off profited from the confidential information by making stock market trades ahead of public corporate announcements. In 2017 he was charged with 13 counts related to insider trading, and as part of a plea deal, he pleaded guilty to one count of conspiring to commit securities fraud. Based on his federal criminal conviction, the Florida Bar found Little in violation of Rule 8.4(b) Misconduct that states: "A lawyer shall not commit a criminal act that reflects adversely on the lawyer's honesty, trustworthiness or fitness as a lawyer in other respects" (American Bar Association 2020). The disciplinary referee noted one aggravating factor (dishonest or selfish motive) along with six mitigating factors including physical or mental disability or impairment.[6] As part of his mitigation for mental disability, Little presented evidence of his mental illness in both his federal court case and his subsequent disciplinary case. His psychiatrist testified:

> It is my opinion that throughout the time frame where the illegal conduct occurred, Mr. Little was misdiagnosed by his treating physician, and prescribed an amphetamine medication that worsened and exacerbated the undiagnosed Bipolar Disorder. Individuals suffering from untreated Bipolar Disorder demonstrate distorted judgment and reasoning, engaging in reckless activity and focused on the pleasure and gratification of the moment, disregarding the long-term and potentially catastrophic consequences of that activity. It is my opinion that the misdiagnosis and treatment with amphetamine/stimulant medications, which worsened Mr. Little's true underlying psychiatric disorder during the timeframe of the misconduct and adversely impacted his judgment and behavior represent factors that the Court may wish to consider in deciding Mr. Little's disposition. (Little 2018, 4)

OUR VIEW

Despite offering evidence of being misdiagnosed and going untreated for a serious mental illness, the court declined to extend mitigation to the attorney because there was no evidence presented showing that the attorney's bipolar disorder caused him to participate in insider trading. It is unclear why the court did not find a link between the symptoms of bipolar disorder—reckless activity and distorted judgment—and insider trading. It appears then that misdiagnosis of an untreated serious mental illness does not mitigate against specific-intent crimes such as felony for conspiracy to commit securities fraud and may not mitigate other similar crimes.

CASE EXAMPLE # 9: *KENTUCKY V. ISENBERG* (2011)

In 2011 attorney Isenberg was suspended for five years from practicing law and ordered to comply with monitoring requirements through the Kentucky Lawyers Assistance Program. Isenberg's suspension stemmed from his work on a 2006 worker's compensation matter where he had "made a series of misrepresentations" to the client about a $20,000 settlement check (*Isenberg* 2011, 329). Isenberg, it was later discovered, had deposited the money into his own account and never sent the client their portion of the settlement. He said he knew "what I was doing was wrong, but at the time I did not care" (*Isenberg* 2011, 329). The client filed a complaint against Isenberg in January 2008 with the Kentucky Bar Association (KBA) where the bar alleged he had violated rules involving communication, mishandling of client funds, failing to send the client money owed from the settlement, and engaging in dishonesty, fraud, deceit, or misrepresentation.

The same month the client reported the attorney to the state bar, Isenberg was hospitalized for over a week due to symptoms of serious mental illness. He was initially treated for depression but upon discharge from the hospital he received an updated diagnosis of bipolar disorder through his outpatient provider. He reported participating in counseling and taking Seroquel which the board noted to be an antipsychotic medication. At his disciplinary hearing, his outpatient treating clinician offered testimony by deposition and in the form of a letter about Isenberg's diagnoses and treatment. She testified that Isenberg's behavior during the time of his misconduct was "consistent" with behaviors typically seen during manic episodes (*Isenberg* 2011, 329). Given Isenberg's mental health symptoms and pending complaint with the bar, he stopped practicing law completely and switched over to teaching. His clinician reported that by the following year his symptoms were "well managed" but that he would continue to need treatment for the rest of his life (*Isenberg* 2011, 330). After the board compared this case to the facts in 2005's *KBA v. Steiner*,[7] the "framework for analyzing appropriate discipline in the context of mental illness" (*Isenberg* 2011, 330), the Trial Commissioner determined Isenberg should receive mitigation for his mental health issues because he had met his burden of proof in showing a connection between his misconduct and his mental illness.

Recommendations for sanctions were split following Isenberg's hearing. In total, 16 Board members attended the hearing; 12 Board members recommended Isenberg receive a five-year suspension, four members advocated for "permanent disbarment," and the Trial Commissioner voted to suspend him for three years (*Isenberg* 2011, 331). Isenberg, for his part, argued for a one-year suspension in light of his mitigating factors. As stated earlier, he ultimately received a five-year suspension but as of 2017 has since been disbarred.

OUR VIEW

Isenberg's case is interesting for several reasons. First, it is promising in that it shows yet another case where an attorney was offered mitigation for mental illness. Here, the evidence presented, namely the treating clinician's testimony, points to Isenberg having experienced a manic episode at the time he was representing a client. Specifically, the clinician's testimony where she opined his depositing of the client's settlement check was consistent with mania indicates she believed he was manic at the time. However, there are limited details surrounding the episode described in the court's opinion so it is unclear when the mania began and/or ended. Although we do not know details leading up to his psychiatric hospitalization, it appears *Isenberg* had been treated for quite some time throughout his life based on the court stating he was treated "for a number of years for anxiety and depression" (*Isenberg* 2011, 329) meaning he was likely treated for unipolar depression. Studies have shown patients with bipolar disorder tend to seek out treatment when experiencing symptoms of depression as opposed to symptoms of mania (Bowden 2005; Hirschfield and Vornik 2004) so there is a chance Isenberg may not have reached out for clinical help in the past when experiencing a manic episode. Misdiagnosis is also fairly common for patients with bipolar disorder. Studies show that almost half of patients with bipolar disorder are first diagnosed with depression (Ghaemi et al. 1999; Ghaemi et al. 2000).

A troubling fact about Isenberg is that the background information offered in the opinion suggests he was alone. It was noted he had left his father's firm in 2000 and was "office sharing" with other attorneys (*Isenberg* 2011, 328). No mention is made of other colleagues helping him through a particularly vulnerable period of his life. Isolated individuals with a history of mental illness, as we know, can mentally decompensate unbeknownst to others around them. It is unfortunate his colleagues whom he shared an office with were unaware of his condition which led to the misconduct. Had he continued practicing at his father's firm, or any other firm for that matter, it is possible other attorneys by way of their reporting duties under Model Rule 5.1(b-c) could have helped identify signs of Isenberg's oncoming illness and possibly prevented harm to the client (e.g., offering additional supervision and support or even removing him from the case).

Additionally, the timing of his hospitalization is striking in that it occurred during the same month the client filed the complaint against him. Client complaints followed by state bar investigations are an incredibly stressful experience for any attorney but may be especially so for those managing serious and chronic forms of mental illness. Emergent crises necessitating hospitalization is a typical characteristic of bipolar disorder; the effects of this can be devastating for attorneys trying to maintain a law practice. Hospitalizations, such as Isenberg's, may likely interrupt an attorney's practice, leading to issues with clients and their cases.

ANXIETY

Another commonly reported mental health disorder in attorney disciplinary cases is anxiety. Anxiety is defined as the "anticipation of future threat" (American Psychiatric Association 2013, 189). Anxiety is a universal human emotion and can be a normal, nonpathological response to stimuli; however, excessive fear and avoidance coupled with clinically significant distress and functional impairment may be diagnosable.

Anxiety disorders comprise an array of mental illnesses involving anxiety such as phobias, social anxiety, generalized anxiety, and panic disorder among others. Anxiety is highly comorbid with depression disorders as well as with one another meaning individuals with an anxiety problem may meet criteria for more than one kind of anxiety disorder (American Psychiatric Association 2013). When individuals say they have anxiety or an anxiety problem, they are using a broad term which may not necessarily mean they have been diagnosed with an anxiety disorder per the DSM-5. In general, such individuals may be referring to Panic Disorder or to the classic diagnosis of Generalized Anxiety Disorder (GAD).

Panic Disorder is typically diagnosed when an individual experiences "recurrent unexpected panic attacks" (American Psychiatric Association 2013, 190). The nature of panic attacks can range; some people may have more frequent panic attacks with greater intensity while others may experience less frequent, less intense ones (American Psychiatric Association 2013). According to the American Psychiatric Association (2013), common characteristics of a panic attack are:

- Tachycardia (pounding heart)
- Chest pains
- Difficulty catching one's breath
- Feeling weak or dizzy
- Sweating
- Feeling as if one is going to die or go crazy

GAD, on the other hand, is characterized by persistent and excessive worry over everyday things. GAD feels less acute than Panic Disorder in that the individual with GAD may feel chronically anxious throughout the days, weeks, and months. The American Psychiatric Association (2013, 2017) states that symptoms of GAD can include the following symptoms:

- Feeling restless
- Feeling on edge or fatigued
- Problems concentrating
- Difficulties with sleeping

There can be many functional impairments for attorneys who have anxiety. Symptoms of "muscle tension. . . feeling keyed up or on edge, tiredness, difficulty concentrating, and disturbed sleep" are well-known to the condition (APA 2013, 190). Anxious attorneys feel like the standard in practice because anxiety and the accompanying stress are so common. Feeling anxious heading into trial or in a contentious argument with a client would likely be a normal physiological and emotional response to a stressful situation. However, attorneys who have an anxiety disorder like GAD would experience ongoing functional impairments in their personal life or at work in addition to experiencing the anxiety as significantly distressing. The following are case examples of attorneys who reported anxiety as a reason for mitigation.

CASE EXAMPLE #10: *IN RE OWENS* (2018)

Owens, an attorney licensed in Kansas and Missouri, was in the middle of completing a diversion program on a prior agreement when the Kansas Board for Discipline of Attorneys became aware of potentially new misconduct. Two of Owens' clients reported complaints against her in Kansas. The first client stated she did not file, nor communicate on the status of, his employment discrimination case. The second client stated she did not return multiple phone calls or emails regarding a change she was supposed to make on a birth certificate; the client ended up hiring a new attorney to complete the work. The Disciplinary Administrator claimed Owens had violated the following Kansas Rules of Professional Conduct: competence, diligence, communication, safekeeping property, and termination of representation among others.

At her disciplinary hearing, Owens presented evidence of an anxiety disorder. She stated her general practitioner (GP) physician had diagnosed her with anxiety 12 days before the hearing, and she was prescribed medication for the condition. She described her anxiety as "often overwhelming" (*Owens* 2018, 94). Owens appeared to blame her misconduct on her problems with anxiety when she testified that it "caused her to be unable to move [the client's] case forward, to terminate properly her representation of [the client], and to cooperate in the investigation of [the client's] complaint" (*Owens* 2018, 86). The Board ultimately agreed with the hearing panel in finding that her anxiety was a mitigating factor because it "significantly contributed to her misconduct" (*Owens* 2018, 87). She received a six-month suspension with a reinstatement condition that required her to obtain treatment for the anxiety disorder.

OUR VIEW

Owens' case shows some jurisdictions are flexible in terms of evidence required to prove mental illness as a mitigating factor. Here, *Owens* received a diagnosis of anxiety a mere 12 days before her hearing with no mention of any previous treatment. As opposed to cases where more lead time is required to prove a mental health condition, the *Owens* court shows that some jurisdictions are willing to accept evidence in the days leading up to the hearing. Furthermore, it is noted in the court's opinion that *Owens* was diagnosed with anxiety by a "general practice physician" (*Owens* 2018, 85). Of course, there are no hard and fast rules stating individuals must be evaluated by mental health professionals, and it is common for patients to seek treatment through their primary care doctors, but as a whole mental health disorders are outside the scope of a GP's practice (Afana et al. 2002; Wittchen et al. 2003). One would think it would be more persuasive for Owens to be seen by a mental health professional, and yet the court was persuaded enough to offer her mitigation for her mental health issues.

In comparison to *Owens*, the case *Erie-Huron Grievance Committee v. Stoll* (2010) offers similar facts with a less favorable outcome. In *Stoll*, the attorney was charged with more than 20 counts of violations for failing to file probate and guardianship documents. He argued during the mitigation phase of his hearing he was in ill health and suffering from years of anxiety and depression. Despite his reports he produced minimal evidence of his conditions; the Ohio Supreme Court noted in its opinion that Stoll solely offered an Ohio Lawyers Assistance Program (OLAP) social worker as a witness. The OLAP clinician testified though she had only met Stoll "days before the panel hearing" (Stoll 2010, 292), she believed he had anxiety and depression. Stoll testified before the Board that his mental health conditions impaired his ability to work. The Board, however, did not consider Stoll's anxiety and depression issues in mitigation and suspended him for two years, or one-and-a-half years longer than Owens. Overall, *Owens* opens up more ways to evaluate and diagnose attorneys who are seeking mitigation for their mental health issues.

CASE EXAMPLE # 11: *IN THE MATTER OF HILL* (2015)

Hill was seen before the Supreme Court of Georgia on a petition he submitted to resolve two former clients' grievances against him. The clients had reported him to the state bar for his handling of their home foreclosure. As part of their initial agreement, the clients had paid Hill $3,000 as part of a retainer and promised to pay him $300 per month for work performed on the foreclosure transactions. After the bank petitioned to remove the case from state to federal court and filed a motion to dismiss, Hill failed to inform the clients of the removal and disabuse them of thinking he was continuing to work on the case. Regrettably, the clients were evicted from their home. Hill admitted to violating Georgia Rules of Professional Conduct on diligence and communication.

Because attorneys licensed in Georgia can request specific disciplinary outcomes through the court, Hill petitioned for an indefinite suspension of his law license of not less than six months based on his mental health issues, meaning he could become eligible for reinstatement after serving six months of the suspension. He reported being in "continual treatment" (*Hill* 2015, 634) for Generalized Anxiety Disorder and depression since 1991, well before he was admitted to the bar in 2008. He reported he ". . . went through a difficult time managing his condition, became overwhelmed, and experienced a paralysis that kept him from taking appropriate actions" (*Hill* 2015, 634–635). The Board approved his petition request for voluntary discipline and suspended him indefinitely.

OUR VIEW

Hill's petition is unique in its vulnerability and description of how anxiety and depression can interact with each other to create an exceptionally stressful experience while practicing law. Faced with an impending foreclosure, it appears *Hill* performed a significant amount of work for the clients he represented in this matter. The court's opinion indicated he stopped interacting with the clients upon the bank's removal to federal court and after "conclud[ing] that the case would not survive the [bank's] motion to dismiss" (*Hill* 2015, 634). Of course, there are limited details regarding Hill's cognitive and emotional processes during this period of time, but it is not too difficult to imagine how hopeless and devastating it must feel to zealously advocate on behalf of your clients only to be hit with the realization you will likely lose the case and your clients will lose their home. Apparently, Hill had been treated in the past for anxiety and depression, two highly comorbid conditions, so it is possible the bad news he received on this particular case triggered a well-worn pattern of intense feelings—what he referred to as "paralysis"—that caused him to feel helpless.

CASE EXAMPLE # 12: *DISCIPLINARY COUNSEL V. ENGEL* (2018)

Ohio attorney Engel was hired by a client in April 2015 to represent her on a debt collection case. Over the course of the next several months, the client attempted to reach Engel to discuss the case but received no follow-up. In August, the client filed a complaint with the state board. Though Engel told the board he would reach out to the client, he did not contact her until February of the following year. By March 2016, the client had notified Engel that she had settled the debt collection herself and requested he return her $500 retainer. The Ohio Disciplinary Board determined he had violated several professional rules of conduct including diligence, communication, withdrawal, and cooperation with the disciplinary investigation. The board recommended a two-year suspension with 18 months stayed.

Engel objected to the board's discipline recommendation and argued for a full stayed suspension based in part on his mental health factors. In mitigation, Engel stated that while working on his client's case he "did not realize he was suffering from anxiety and depression or that his conditions were adversely affecting his practice," and he was "incredibly ashamed of and embarrassed by his conduct..." (*Engel* 2018, 2013). He reported that in addition to entering into a three-year monitoring contract with the Ohio Lawyers Assistance Program (OLAP), he started seeing a psychologist for therapy sessions in August 2016 and began taking an antidepressant. His therapist testified through written and video testimony that Engel had suffered from mental health issues for several years and "tended to avoid conflict, isolate himself, and shut down emotionally" (*Engel* 2018, 2014). She gauged his improvement post-treatment as at least 75 percent better than when he initially started. She opined that his mental health "contributed significantly" to delays on his client's case but that she could not articulate why he encountered these issues on only one particular case and not the rest of his workload (*Engel* 2018, 2013). Ultimately the board reaffirmed its decision to suspend Engel. The Board argued that they had considered his mental health as a mitigating factor but that it was not enough to overcome the aggravating factors (prior misconduct, multiple offenses, noncooperation). The Board reasoned that without taking his mental health into consideration, Engel likely would have been suspended indefinitely.

OUR VIEW

In this case, the attorney stated he did not recognize how his own mental health symptoms were affecting him. Often, individuals suffering from mental health issues can exhibit limited insight into their symptoms, making it difficult to identify the impact of the illness(es) on functioning. Attorneys in particular may be more susceptible to being blind to mental health symptoms given the nature of attorney work culture. Likewise, it is possible that Engel did not recognize specific factors about that particular client case that triggered his misconduct. As the Disciplinary Board pointed out, it is curious as to why Engel only exhibited problems with one case and not his entire caseload. Perhaps the Board expected to see more global impairment when it comes to mental health disorders; however, oftentimes individuals with anxiety issues can become quite triggered by certain relationships or events that are unconscious and outside of awareness. Thus, some aspects of a mental health disorder may go unanswered at the time of a disciplinary hearing.

CASE EXAMPLE #13: *IN THE MATTER OF KUPKA* (2020)

Law firm associate Kupka began working at a Kansas firm in 2011. During her employment she performed a range of duties including litigating, serving as city prosecutor, managing limited action dockets, and supporting colleagues in the firm on other matters. She was for the most part unsupervised; she denied being designated a supervising attorney and her interaction with mentors was infrequent due to "routine[. . .] cancel[ations]" (*Kupka* 2020, 244). Four years after joining the firm she inherited a colleague's family law practice which was an unfamiliar area of the law.

Kupka also tried to maintain a life outside of the office. In her personal life, she became engaged while working at the firm but believed taking time off of work was discouraged. In fact, she "took no time off the week of her wedding and had a very short honeymoon" before returning to work (*Kupka* 2020, 244). She became pregnant in 2017. She had anticipated her workload would scale down during the pregnancy but it "grew rapidly" after a partner and two paralegals went out on leave (*Kupka* 2020, 245). She "struggled to get organized but files were everywhere, papers were everywhere and notes were everywhere" (*Kupka* 2002, 245). The work "overwhelmed her to the point that she would 'sit there and stare at it and just be paralyzed'" (*Kupka* 2020, 245). Her work suffered; she provided false statements to clients and colleagues regarding work she had done on several matters; she claimed to have filed documents when she had not. In one case she "falsified the judge's signature and court's filed-stamp on the judgment" (*Kupka* 2020, 245). Upon becoming aware of her misconduct, the firm investigated all of the work she had performed at the firm. Both she and the firm reported her misconduct to the Kansas State Bar for further handling. The court noted she stipulated to violations of competence, diligence, communication, truthfulness, and dishonesty among others.

Before the Board, Kupka presented evidence of mental health issues for consideration in her disciplinary case. In addition to reporting feeling "overwhelmed and overworked" (*Kupka* 2020, 249), she stated she experienced anxiety and depression issues which she sought treatment for. She further informed the Board she had initiated a monitoring agreement with the Kansas Lawyers Assistance Program (KALAP) as part of her recovery plan. The board discussed her mental health issues as a mitigating factor[8] in the court opinion but also characterized her conduct during her employment as indicative of a dishonest motive. Ultimately, Kupka was suspended for two years with a recommendation to be reinstated after serving six months of suspension time.

OUR VIEW

Kupka's case represents a somewhat infamous and classic tale in law firm lore of the overworked and under-supported associate attorney. It appears she began her career at the firm right after graduating from law school. She performed a variety of work in diverse matters with, as she had reported to the board, little oversight. It is of course no secret that working as a new associate for a firm is stressful; many associates either leave or burnout after discovering the path to making partner is not for them. Notwithstanding the law firm employment experience, it seems a combination of several factors contributed to Kupka's mental and emotional deterioration.

One of the more salient factors in this case is a familiar storyline for women attorneys who have struggled to carve out a personal life amidst all of the paperwork. Practicing law can be especially stressful for women during a period of their lives where the added pressure of marriage and children is commonplace. Some articles in fact even advocate against getting married while working in law (Chen 2020; Gillespie 2021). With a high prevalence rate of divorce at almost 27 percent for attorneys (Ly et al. 2015), it seems clear what the effects of working in a stressful environment can do to relationships. In Kupka's case, it appears she was at a developmental stage in her life where she was trying to balance multiple needs; she worked diligently for several years at the firm, as evidenced by the various matters she took on throughout her employment, while juggling an engagement, wedding, and childrearing. She was, as she stated, under the impression she could not take time off from work for herself. Given the amount of work law firm associates handle and the high billing requirements typically in place, it is not unusual for associates to forgo taking vacations or even their own weddings as in this case. As mentioned before, the amount of work, stress, and pressure placed on associates can be detrimental from a mental health perspective and can lead to compassion fatigue, burnout, and many other mental health conditions.

Here, Kupka reported experiencing anxiety and depression in relation to her workload. The court's opinion mentions she received treatment for her conditions, in addition to participating in a formal monitoring program through KALAP, but it did not explicitly describe her diagnoses or treatment. It also appears there was no expert or character testimony on her behalf. Kupka represented herself in the disciplinary matter and testified regarding her mental health. No requests were made by the Board for further information on her mental health treatment so it appears the Board accepted her statements along with the report of her KALAP agreement as mitigation for her misconduct.

CASE EXAMPLE #14: *IN THE MATTER OF ROMANO* (2015)

In a California case, real estate attorney Romano asked for leniency on misconduct stemming from 82 bankruptcy filings made in bad faith. She reported feeling anxious about possibly having a serious medical condition and that her mother needed surgery. Though the attorney had been seeing a psychologist for treatment for six months, the court assigned no weight to the psychologist's opinions in part because it was offered in the form of a letter. The court went on to reason:

> We do not assign any mitigating credit for Romano's emotional difficulties because no clear and convincing evidence establishes that they were directly responsible for her misconduct. Romano's therapist's letter indicated that two main factors contributed to her misconduct—life and health circumstances and her tendency to represent the "underdog." In 2010, Romano was distracted, anxious, and distressed by symptoms she experienced indicating she might have breast or cervical cancer, and because her mother became ill, eventually requiring open-heart surgery. However, Romano filed her first improper bankruptcy petition in 2008, well before she and her mother developed medical issues. Thus, she failed to establish the nexus between her emotional difficulties and her misconduct. (*Romano* 2015, 9)

Essentially, the court stated that because they had found 82 improperly-filed bankruptcy petitions on behalf of her clients prior to the onset of Romano's reported anxiety, the attorney failed to establish a nexus between her mental health issues and her misconduct and therefore no mitigation should be provided. Romano was disbarred in 2016 almost 30 years to the day after she was admitted to the California bar.

OUR VIEW

This case offers an important perspective on the timing of mental health issues. It appears in this case that the court would have preferred to see an overlap of ongoing health issues and misconduct in order to infer an interaction between the two. The fact that Romano's mental health treatment occurred after the bankruptcy petitions were filed somehow indicated to the court that she could not have experienced problems with anxiety before the start date of her treatment. This assumption that the start of mental health treatment always coincides with the onset of a mental health condition is troubling and threatens the livelihood of attorneys who may not be able to afford treatment or may be unaware of their problems and/or treatment options at the time.

Further, though Romano's treating psychologist submitted a letter on her behalf, the court disregarded the evidence. The court criticized Romano for "only [being] in treatment for six months," not presenting the psychologist in person as a witness, and for offering the psychologist's "three-paragraph letter that had little, if any, persuasive value. . ." This harsh critique from the court implies that courts ascribe little value to shorter-term treatment[9] and requires in-person oral testimony by witnesses.

POSTTRAUMATIC STRESS DISORDER (PTSD)

Most lay people may be familiar with the term Posttraumatic stress disorder, or PTSD. PTSD is a mental health diagnosis that arose to describe the cluster of symptoms seen in soldiers returning from war. PTSD has gone by other names such as battle fatigue and shell shock. Although PTSD originated from times of war, sufferers of PTSD are a diverse group of people that expand far beyond combat veterans. The disorder is part of the trauma and stressor-related disorders section of the DSM-5 and is characterized by an onset of specific symptoms subsequent to a trauma (American Psychiatric Association 2013). Over the years as we have come to better understand the disorder, the criteria for PTSD have evolved. Symptoms of PTSD involve:

- Intrusive thoughts, memories, dreams, or flashbacks
- A desire to avoid the people, places, or things that are reminders of the event
- Changes in mood or thoughts, e.g., feeling guilty, ashamed, alienated, dissociated, or thinking you are the reason the event occurred
- Changes in activity, e.g., being more hypervigilant or easy to startle, feeling irritable

From what we know of PTSD, the symptoms can present in a rather diffuse manner that may come and go and be difficult to discern from other mental health disorders. Comorbidity is common too with PTSD where individuals experience an estimated 80 percent greater likelihood of meeting criteria for another mental health disorder when compared to non-PTSD individuals (American Psychiatric Association 2013).

PTSD can affect attorneys in a variety of ways. It may show up primarily as anxiety; the attorney may be plagued with poor sleep due to nightmares which may come and go unpredictably. Sleep difficulties can make an individual with PTSD more prone to experiencing other symptoms. Some attorneys may cope through avoidance of stimuli.

CASE EXAMPLE #15: *IN RE SALO* (2012)

New York attorney Salo was reported to New York's State Bar for mismanaging and commingling his client's $200k personal injury settlement. While holding onto a portion of the settlement money in his client trust account, the New York court found he had allowed the balance on the account to drop to $102.88. Salo did not argue against the facts of the case and instead presented significant evidence that his misconduct was due to "[PTSD] and depression, stemming from childhood abuse and from his proximity to the September 11, 2001, attacks on the World Trade Center in New York" (*Salo* 2012, 176). He argued that his mental health issues prevented him from forming the intent necessary to engage in the misconduct. The experts he presented stated that because of his PTSD:

[]which caused him to stop opening mail, including bank statements[. . .], [he] lost track of the fact that the balance remaining in his [Interest on Lawyer Account] IOLA account was subject to the lien on the proceeds of the settlement, and believed that he was drawing on the "cushion" of earned legal fees it was his practice to keep in the account. (*Salo* 2012, 177)

New York determined Salo's expert testimony was "uncontroverted" and found he did not have the "venal intent required for a finding that he willfully and knowingly converted third-party funds" (*Salo* 2010, 22). The court found him to be merely responsible for negligent misappropriation which carried a different, albeit lesser, punishment. The New York court accordingly determined that a one-year suspension was an appropriate sanction based on the evidence presented.

Salo, who was also licensed to practice law in the District of Columbia at the time of this case, self-reported his New York discipline to the D.C. Office of Bar Counsel. D.C. noted that had the same misconduct emerged from their jurisdiction, the D.C. court would have "deemed it reckless or intentional misappropriation warranting automatic disbarment. . ." but would have likely applied mitigation to stay the disbarment (*Salo* 2012, 179). After considering the facts presented in the New York court, the D.C. Court of Appeals suspended Salo from practicing law for a period of six months for his misconduct.

OUR VIEW

This case illustrates an example of how mitigation for a mental health disorder can affect a reciprocal action in another jurisdiction. As stated previously, attorneys are subject to reciprocal discipline in any jurisdiction they are licensed. It appears here Salo benefited from his case originating out of New York because he received mitigation for his PTSD, and he was able to use that evidence for a lighter sentence on his reciprocal D.C. case.

This case is also noteworthy for shedding light on the lasting traumatic effects some attorneys experienced in the aftermath of 9/11. New York was, and still remains, the most densely populated state for attorneys with many working in Manhattan in and around the surrounding area of where the World Trade Center once stood. Although this is one of the few cases we have reviewed where an attorney presented evidence of PTSD triggered by 9/11, we would not be surprised to hear if other attorneys had also experienced difficulty at work given the proximity of the attacks to law firms in the city.

In addition to 9/11, Salo mentioned another detail which appeared related to the trauma of the terrorist attacks: childhood abuse. We note this because oftentimes individuals who present with PTSD after experiencing traumatic events may have endured previous unresolved traumas in childhood (Zaidi and Foy 1994). Additional trauma in adulthood may compound already existing issues in vulnerable individuals, making them more likely to experience adverse mental health outcomes.[10] In this case, Salo may have been more prone to developing mental health issues due to his past history of abuse.

CASE EXAMPLE #16: *IN THE MATTER OF AMPONSAH* (2019)

In another PTSD case, a California attorney who commingled funds with his client and inappropriately used client trust accounts to pay his own bills presented evidence of PTSD and "severe anxiety" related to his battle over a personal child custody matter. He testified he was in a "mental fog" over his 2017 suspension due to worrying that he would lose custody of his six-year-old daughter because he could not earn a living. The court noted, "He testified that he functioned by taking one thing at a time as he was 'trying to focus on survival.' He lost weight, experienced tremors, and became withdrawn, as witnessed by his friends. . ." (*Amponsah* 2019, 9).

At his hearing Amponsah offered testimony from a colleague and his treating psychologist. His colleague testified as to observing Amponsah "sit in a dark office for hours—a marked change from the detailed and organized attorney who had been his partner for more than two decades" (*Amponsah* 2019, 9). His psychologist who had known him since 2006 testified about the course of his mental health treatment. She offered "detailed facts about his emotional difficulties" in 2017, during the time of the misconduct, and testified the attorney experienced significant distress over his child custody case and "extreme fear of losing [. . .] his daughter" (*Amponsah* 2019, 10). The psychologist reported the attorney's condition had significantly gotten better and described him as "a healthy man today. . . ." (*Amponsah* 2019, 10). In response to the evidence offered by the attorney, the sentencing court actually increased the amount of mitigation initially offered during the hearing judge's culpability determination, and the attorney avoided disbarment by receiving a suspension of two years.

OUR VIEW

In this case it appears the state court found a sympathetic attorney who warranted more mitigation than what was initially recommended, a feat few disciplined attorneys ever achieve. In fact, Amponsah was found to have several aggravating factors (prior discipline record, multiple acts of misconduct, indifference), yet he was still able to receive mitigation for his reported extreme emotional difficulties in spite of the Office of Chief Trial Counsel of the State Bar's recommendation that he be disbarred. It appears that the court in this case was particularly persuaded by Amponsah's harrowing descriptions of his emotional state which were corroborated by his coworker's and long-time therapist's testimony. Thus, the effective testimony of three individuals (the attorney, a coworker, the treating therapist) was able to overcome the mitigation requirements of Standard 1.6(d). Of importance, the treating therapist provided detailed facts about Amponsah's emotional problems during the time of the misconduct.

Amponsah's success in his state bar hearing raises the question as to whether other attorneys should attempt to emulate what he did in their disciplinary hearings to ensure mitigation. What Amponsah did, of course, may prove very difficult for others as it requires having at least one colleague who actually witnessed the attorney's emotional decompensation and is willing to testify regarding this eyewitness account. It also requires that the attorney have a longstanding therapeutic relationship reaching back years before any discipline action is initiated (it was stated that Amponsah had been in treatment with his therapist since 2006 which would be about 10 years prior to his 2016 commingling of funds). This configuration may not be feasible for other attorneys, especially those at the start of their careers who do not have enough history with colleagues and/or other professionals who can testify on the attorney's behalf.

CASE EXAMPLE #17: *IN RE PERRICONE* (2018)

Before his disciplinary action, veteran attorney Perricone worked in private practice, as a special agent in the FBI, and then as an AUSA for the Eastern District of Louisiana. His work in the field was described as "exemplary" by peers (*Perricone* 2018, 7). But in 2012 he was forced to resign from the position of Chief Litigation Counsel after it was discovered he authored thousands of anonymous posts under five usernames begrudging pending legal cases in the comments section of a New Orleans newspaper website. His identity was eventually uncovered by a linguistics expert who noticed similarities in words used in the anonymous posts and in his filed briefs through the office of the U.S. Attorney. One federal judge even alluded to the attorney's posts as evidence of prosecutorial misconduct before ordering a new trial in the infamous Danzinger Bridge case (National Public Radio 2015).

In his defense, Perricone explained that his online posting was intended to be a form of positive coping. He reported thinking it "would help him deal with the stress of his work as a U.S. Attorney" but that it ended up "exacerbat[ing] his stress and anxiety" (*Perricone* 2018, 314). He testified that the origins of his stress and anxiety reached back to his work in law enforcement. His clinical psychologist diagnosed him with PTSD stemming from "numerous situations" he endured including witnessing the "gruesome deaths of others" and having his life threatened by gunfire (*Perricone* 2018, 314).

The court, however, had a difficult time connecting the attorney's PTSD to the behavior that led to his misconduct. During his expert's testimony, the court offered these criticisms:

[The psychologist] based his opinion entirely on what Respondent had told him, but, while he had administered some psychological testing of Respondent, he had administered no tests for Respondent's credibility, such as the Minnesota Multi-Phasic Personality Inventory [MMPI]. The Committee found credible Respondent's testimony that he was under a great deal of stress at work, especially in the period following Hurricane Katrina, when public corruption being investigated by the U.S. Attorney's office was rampant. The Committee was skeptical of Dr. Cambias's diagnosis of PTSD and its causative role in Respondent's blogging, but no countervailing opinion testimony was offered. (*Perricone* 2018, 9)

OUR VIEW

It is uncommon in our research to see a disciplinary court recommend a specific type of psychological testing such as the MMPI as mentioned above. In general, the MMPI's uses have been to aid clinical diagnosis and "assess major symptoms of social and personal maladjustment" (Pearson 2021). The MMPI does contain validity scales which could be what the court was alluding to when it suggested that the attorney's expert should have administered the test to address "credibility," but that recommendation along with the rest of the court's tone in analyzing the expert testimony indicates a negative view of the attorney's evidence. To suggest the attorney undergo a psychological test to determine credibility implies a lack of credibility about the information presented, not to mention that the court expressly stated they were "skeptical" of the psychologist's testimony.

Though Perricone's testifying psychologist opined that Perricone's PTSD diagnosis and mental health issues led him to engage in the misconduct at issue, the Disciplinary Board rejected his attempts to use his mental health problems in mitigation. The Board specifically pointed to the psychologist's testimony wherein he stated that Perricone, despite his mental health issues, is capable of "operat[ing] at a high level" and "knew right from wrong" (*Perricone* 2018, 318). Using language similar to the requirements under insanity, the Board dismissed Perricone's mental health testimony as not meeting the causation element under the ABA's Standard 9.32(i)(2) and reasoned they found more credibility in Perricone's testimony by stating:

When asked why he engaged in commenting in a prohibited way, respondent candidly admitted that he was angry over public corruption and he vented this anger in the caustic criticism leveled against all who, in his judgment, warranted accountability, even though he knew this was improper. . . . Respondent's own testimony reveals he was aware that he should not post these comments, yet he decided to do so anyway. Clearly, any mental disability from which respondent suffered did not prevent him from knowing his actions were wrong. Under these circumstances, we find absolutely no support for the conclusion that respondent has proven his mental condition caused the misconduct. Accordingly, we decline to consider his mental disability in mitigation. (*Perricone* 2018, 318–319)

Though the majority of the hearing committee recommended a two-year suspension, Perricone was disbarred from practicing in Louisiana as a result of this case. The court added: "Our decision today must send a strong message to respondent and to all the members of the bar that a lawyer's ethical obligations are not diminished by the mask of anonymity provided by the internet" (*Perricone* 2018, 319).

As noted above, the court wanted to make an example out of Perricone for engaging in misconduct, and they disbarred him rather than accepting the recommendation of suspension by the hearing court. The opinion as well as the language of the court is punitive and condemning. It may not have mattered what his treating psychologist testified to if the court was set on punishing Perricone so harshly so as to deter others from engaging in the same conduct, but it is notable that Perricone's psychologist's testimony, which may have likely met the burden of proof by other courts' standards, was rejected.

There also appeared to be an emphasis on Perricone's knowledge of right and wrong. His "knowing" about or being "aware" that posting such comments was inappropriate seemed particularly interesting, as if his defense hinged upon ignorance of prosecutorial standards or that mental health disorders mean that the individual is ignorant of ethical standards. Perhaps the fact that he appeared "high-functioning" also precluded him from qualifying for mental health mitigation in this court. Clearly, Perricone was an aware and functioning attorney who knew his behavior was wrong and did it anyway, as stated throughout the decision, but these are not the standards that should be imposed on individuals requesting mitigation for mental health issues. Courts, instead, should adhere to the standards laid out by the ABA's guidelines or through their own line of state stare decisis when determining mitigation to ensure consistency in mitigation factors.

CASE EXAMPLE #18: *MARYLAND V. MILLER* (2020)

In another case where the judge rejected a diagnosis of PTSD and its connections to misconduct, Maryland attorney Miller testified as to her mental health problems. In her disciplinary hearing for violating several rules under Maryland Attorneys' Rules of Professional Conduct (MARPC) in an adoption case, Miller reported she had suffered physical, emotional, and sexual abuse by family members as a child and had been diagnosed with PTSD.[11] She produced two witnesses, one licensed professional mental health counselor, and one forensic psychiatrist, who opined as to Miller's mental health status.

Miller argued several points about her PTSD which were repeatedly rejected by the hearing judge. At one point, she stated that her PTSD was triggered after a contentious phone call with the client one night in February 2016. At trial, Miller's psychiatrist "testified that the trigger could likely be based on an overreaction by [Ms. Miller] to an imaginary fear regarding [the client]" (Miller 2020, 997). The court, however, stated that "the question of whether some imagined slight could have caused the misconduct is irrelevant" and found her testimony regarding the phone call to be incredible before rejecting it. The hearing judge stated, "While the court is deeply sympathetic towards [Ms. Miller's] traumatic experiences and mental health diagnosis, the court rejects that [Ms. Miller's] PTSD was triggered because the court is not persuaded that the February 2016 conflict occurred between [the client] and [Ms. Miller]" (*Miller* 2020, 996).

Miller also testified that because of her PTSD, she "structured her practice in a way that has allowed her to avoid relationships with difficult clients or those that would likely result in disputes." This testimony was rejected due to the hearing judge perceiving that through Miller's part-time work as a panel attorney for the public defender, she could not pick and choose which clients she works with and therefore could not "avoid interaction with contentious clients."

Upon review, the Maryland Court of Appeals agreed with the hearing judge's findings on Miller's mental health by stating:

> In the instant grievance proceedings, Ms. Miller's PTSD does not rise to the level of "compelling extenuating mitigation[,]" because she failed to establish that it met the "root cause" standard. . . . Accordingly, given the multitude of violations of the MARPC, Ms. Miller engaged in and the overarching dishonesty undergirding a substantial number of these violations, disbarment is the only appropriate sanction. (*Miller* 2020, 998)

OUR VIEW

PTSD commonly involves hypervigilance where an "imagined slight" can be very real for the individual who is on the lookout for threats. It is not uncommon to have vastly differing experiences of the same stimuli. The dilemma then for courts may lie in the perceived forced choice aspect of testimony; they can side with one litigant or the other but not both. Needless to say, it is inherently problematic to dismiss an individual, especially one who presents evidence of an extensive trauma history.

Here, it appears the judge received disputed evidence over what occurred in a phone conversation; the client viewed the conversation as innocuous whereas the attorney, who reported having an extensive history of trauma, observed the interaction as threatening. The hearing judge in this case ultimately rejected the attorney's testimony. From a mental health perspective, the judge may have unknowingly reenacted the role of an aggressor and/ or retraumatized the attorney by invalidating her claims. Of course, fear of retraumatizing fragile individuals is not reason to shy away from making a difficult decision, but we would urge anyone involved in making such decisions to consider the possibility that what a litigant testifies to under oath is real.

CASE EXAMPLE #19: *IN RE WEBB* (2018)

Solo practitioner Webb opened up a law practice in Oregon in 2011. She managed the law office, which included all of the finances, on her own. Between 2014 and 2015, around the time she started having money problems of her own, Webb mismanaged three separate client trust accounts. In the first case, she "falsely" told the client their $6,000 settlement check had been mailed when it had not (*Webb* 2018, 4). She sent a check to the client even though there was not enough money in the client trust account to cover the amount of the check. She told the Oregon State Bar at the time that she had mean to send a different amount to the client. In the second client case, Webb received a $70,000 settlement check of which $44,000 was to go to the client. She depleted the trust account by making withdrawals to pay for personal expenses and other client settlements she had not paid yet. When Webb finally did send the client her $44,000 check, the bank refused to honor the payment because of insufficient funds and charged the client an overdraft fee. In the third client matter, Webb received a $100,000 settlement payment which she used to pay the previous client she owed $52,000 in total. Essentially she paid what was owed one client with the settlement proceeds she received from another client. The Oregon State Bar alleged she misappropriated client funds under the rules for safekeeping property and misconduct.

With respect to relevant mental health issues, she reported experiencing significant symptoms during her representation in the third case where she was supposed to pay the client $46,000 as part of his settlement. She suffered a concussion in a car accident in the middle of the client's trial and was soon after hospitalized for suicidal ideation. She was diagnosed with Major Depressive Disorder and then later with PTSD. She testified her PTSD reached back to events which began in her adolescence. She stated she was also influenced by the events of 9/11 due to being in Washington, D.C., on the day of the attacks and "see[ing] the smoke from. . . the Pentagon" (*Webb* 2018, 5). She stated she "always struggled around the anniversary of the attacks and that, beginning around September 11, 2014, she suffered symptoms of her depression and PTSD that were triggered both by her memories of the terrorist attack and by her financial difficulties" (*Webb* 2018, 5). Her treating psychologist testified regarding her mental health status at her disciplinary hearing. He offered "if [Webb] was under an 'overwhelming amount of stress,' then the symptoms of her untreated mental conditions likely 'caused her enough distress to perhaps influence or cause her to do something that she normally would not have done' if she were managing her stressors 'in an appropriate or adaptive way'" (*Webb* 2018, 5).

When asked about her impairment level at the time of her misconduct (before she entered into treatment), Webb's psychologist had difficulty answering the question. He reported having to rely on her self-reports to him and refused to opine as to her functional impairments in the months leading up to her treatment. He stated "it's possible" to being asked whether she was impaired at the time of her misconduct but declined to affirmatively state that she was (*Webb* 2018, 11).

Following Webb's expert testimony, the Oregon State Bar argued her mental health issues were not a "substantial contributing cause" to her misconduct within the meaning of Standard 9.32(i) by rebutting Webb's expert with their own expert (*Webb* 2018, 9). The Bar put a psychologist who had "reviewed [Webb's] treatment records but did not examine her" on the stand (*Webb* 2018, 5). The Bar's psychologist opined that based on the results of an assessment Webb had completed while being treated for depression and PTSD, he found the results "essentially within normal range" and fairly unanticipated given her testimony regarding her experience of serious mental health symptoms (*Webb* 2018, 5).

In their analysis, the Board determined Webb had not met her burden of proof with respect to showing her mental health condition contributed to her misconduct. The Board explained she had failed to prove the element of causation under Standard 9.32(i) because she did not show "her disability deprived her of 'the ability to appreciate the wrongfulness' of intentionally misappropriating client funds." The Board pointed to her psychologist's unwillingness to testify as to her functional impairment at the time of her misconduct as well as to the Bar's expert who called attention to Webb's high-functioning behavior patterns which they argued demonstrated her lack of impairment. Ultimately Webb ended up being disbarred for her misconduct.

OUR VIEW

This case is troubling for several reasons. The primary reason being that it appears an attorney who had experienced significant mental health issues (not to mention possible physical issues as well given her concussion from a car accident) and presented expert testimony as to her conditions could not persuade the Board. The Board, as they stated, hinged their determination for mitigation on Webb's ability to prove causation in her misconduct. It is unfortunate they based their decision in part on her treating psychologist's unwillingness to testify under oath about her level of functioning during a time when he did not observe her. Mental health professionals, especially those who regularly testify as expert witnesses, are trained to be circumspect in how they describe patients. Clinicians, such as Webb's psychologist, may refuse to unequivocally speculate as to a patient condition or in response to queries about unknowable facts. Thus, when attorney-patients seeking expert testimony request a mental health expert to testify on their behalf, the expert may not offer the kind of testimony the attorney, or the court for that matter, is seeking.

COMPASSION FATIGUE

In 2018 compassion fatigue was added as a potential mitigating factor in attorney discipline. The following case is presented as one in which compassion fatigue was introduced in mitigation of misconduct.

CASE EXAMPLE #20: *IN RE WAECHTER* (2018)

Personal injury attorney Waechter, licensed since 1991, opened a solo practice in 2010. His paralegal managed the practice's finances up until leaving the firm. Thereafter, Waechter began handling his own lawyer trust account and firm operating account. In his handling of the accounts, Waechter was found to have improperly transferred funds from his trust account to the operating account, converted client funds, failed to provide an accurate written accounting, failed to pay parties, and misrepresented his fees. In an accompanying matter the hearing officer for the Washington State Bar Association Disciplinary Board found Waechter had forged his nephew's signature on an insurance payment for a car accident. The hearing officer found four aggravating factors (dishonest or selfish motive, pattern of misconduct, multiple offenses, substantial experience in the practice of law) and four mitigating factors (absence of prior discipline, full and free disclosure to the board, good character or reputation, remorse). The hearing officer contemplated emotional problems as an additional mitigating factor in the case but ultimately rejected it due to insufficient evidence. After considering the facts of the case and weighing the factors, the hearing officer recommended the attorney be disbarred.

Waechter appealed the hearing officer's decision, arguing that the Board should have considered his emotional problems for mitigation purposes and that he should be afforded suspension with monitoring instead of disbarment. His psychologist testified at the hearing that he was "impacted by vicarious traumatization" or compassion fatigue due to losing several personal injury cases in a row and becoming too involved in his clients' cases (*Waechter* 2018, 834). The psychologist said these setbacks led to *Waechter*'s carelessness and difficulty maintaining his firm finances. The Board agreed with the attorney's reasoning that his emotional problems should have been taken into account but stated that the mitigating factor bears "little weight" in any event (*Waechter* 2018, 836). The Board clarified that compassion fatigue did not cause Mr. *Waechter* per se to engage in professional misconduct, that it "merely impacted" him according to his psychologist, and thus he was not entitled to much mitigation because of this (*Waechter* 2018, 834). The Board also declined to stray from the hearing officer's disbarment recommendation due to the Board's unanimous endorsement for disbarment. Waechter was subsequently disbarred from the State of Washington.

OUR VIEW

In this case, the Board considered compassion fatigue as a mitigating factor. Compassion fatigue is not a diagnosable mental health disorder at this time and thus attorneys who use it to justify mitigation would likely argue for it under the category of "emotional problems" or a similar mitigating factor.

Waechter is yet another example of a case where the Board paid close attention to the expert's testimony as they searched for signs indicating direct causation of misconduct. It appears the Board (mis)interpreted the psychologist's use of the passive phrase "impacted by" to mean "merely impacted," an indication of how weak they perceived the nexus between Waechter's compassion fatigue and misconduct. Indeed, the Board's rephrasing of the psychologist's wording connotes a poor connection to behavior, as if to say compassion fatigue sort of contributed to but certainly did not solely cause the misconduct. It would therefore likely behoove mental health clinicians who testify on causation elements to be aware of their word choice when opining on a patient's mental health status and history.

NOTES

1. In comparison to Summers, in Iowa v. Kennedy (2013) the attorney there reported being so debilitated by depression she could not "answer the phone even like when my son would call. I couldn't go to the post office. . . . I couldn't write a letter or mail a letter. . . . I just froze and I absolutely just couldn't do it. I had trouble leaving the house" (666).

2. Aggravating factors noted were multiple offenses causing harm to the client, dishonest motive, a pattern of misconduct, and engaging in deceptive practices.

3. The board noted his mitigating factors were absence of a prior disciplinary record, attempts to make restitution, and good character and reputation.

4. Subsections (a) through (d) of Gov. Bar R. V(13)(C)(7) state: "The following shall not control the discretion of the Board, but may be considered in favor of recommending a less severe sanction: (7) Existence of a disorder when there has been all of the following: (a) A diagnosis of a disorder by a qualified health care professional or qualified chemical dependency professional; (b) A determination that the disorder contributed to cause the misconduct; (c) In the case of mental disorder, a sustained period of successful treatment or in the case of substance use disorder or nonsubstance-related disorder, a certification of successful completion of an approved treatment program; (d) A prognosis from a qualified health care professional or qualified chemical dependency professional that the attorney will be able to return to competent, ethical professional practice under specified conditions."

5. The court recognized that Person had practiced for almost 50 years by the time of this complaint, he had no substantial prior disciplinary history, cooperated with the state bar investigation, exhibited remorse, and maintains a good reputation in the community.

6. See Florida Standard 9.32(h) under Standards for Imposing Law Sanctions.

7. The attorney in KBA v. Steiner (2005) had presented evidence of grief and alcohol issues at his disciplinary trial but was ultimately disbarred for converting client funds in over 100 transactions.

8. Kansas referred to this mitigation factor under their "Personal or Emotional Problems if Such Misfortunes Have Contributed to Violation of the Kansas Rules of Professional Conduct."

9. It appears the court commented on the length of time Romano spent in treatment as a way to explain the psychologist's limitations in providing an opinion on her mental health problems. Although it is not stated in the court order, the number of appointments Romano attended as well as the frequency of therapy appointments would be helpful to know. For example, a patient who attends weekly therapy appointments for six months receives far less treatment than a patient who attends two, three, four, or five appointments a week in that same six-month period. It should also be noted that brief treatments such as Cognitive-Behavioral Therapy (CBT) and Time-Limited Dynamic Psychotherapy (TLDP) have been shown to be effective at addressing issues related to anxiety. Additionally, it should be noted that many therapists operate under a managed-care model with time constraints on treatment which could affect how long patients choose to remain in therapy.

10. This concept is commonly referred to in the law as the eggshell plaintiff.

11. She also reported being diagnosed with Major Depressive Disorder and Passive Personality Disorder; however, these conditions were not the subject of her mental health mitigation strategy.

Chapter 5

Substance Use in the Legal Profession

With attorneys, there are several opportunities to use substances and perhaps just as many ways to cover up problems. Networking events, after-hour meetings, happy hours, drinks with clients, in-between meeting breaks, or an end-of-the-day reward are just some examples of situations which may include one or more substances. Eilene Zimmerman, the ex-wife of a California attorney who died from complications related to his intravenous use of cocaine and opioids, said her husband used to explain his substance-related symptoms by saying, "'I'm sorry. I was in a meeting and I left my phone in my office. That's why you couldn't reach me.' Or, 'We had a client emergency and I was at the client's office. I couldn't get out'—they all seemed plausible" (Zimmerman 2020). Unfortunately for Ms. Zimmerman's ex-husband it was too late; she discovered him alone and deceased from endocarditis in his posh Southern California home.

Although several books[1] about attorneys with substance use disorders have been published, substance use and misuse remains untreated, undertreated, or unrecognized in the legal community.

SUBSTANCE USE DISORDER IN THE DSM-5 (SUDS)

The American Psychiatric Association's *Diagnostic and Statistical Manual of Mental Disorders Fifth Edition* (DSM-5) section entitled "Substance-Related and Addictive Disorders" discusses substance-induced disorders and substance use disorders, the latter of which are the focus of this chapter. Substance Use Disorder (SUD) may be diagnosed for a range of substances including: alcohol, cannabis, hallucinogens, inhalants, opioids, sedatives, hypnotics, anxiolytics, stimulants, tobacco, and other known substances (American Psychiatric Association 2013). Additionally, gambling disorder is now a diagnosable condition in the DSM-5. Although presentation of dependence or addiction under these various substances may vary depending on the individual's symptoms, in general criteria for a SUD is based on the following:

- Taking substances in larger amounts or longer periods of time than intended
- Ineffective efforts to discontinue or decrease use
- Spending a great deal of time obtaining, using, or recovering from the substance
- Craving as manifested by an intense desire or urge for the substance may occur
- Failure to fulfill major role obligations at work, school, or home
- Persistent or recurrent social or interpersonal problems caused or made worse by effects of the substance
- Important social, occupational, or recreational activities are given up or reduced
- Withdrawal from family activities and hobbies to use the substance
- Using in situations that are physically hazardous
- Using despite knowledge of a problem caused by or exacerbated by the substance
- Developing a tolerance
- Experiencing withdrawal symptoms (American Psychiatric Association 2013)

Individuals can be diagnosed with more than one SUD. Certain SUDs, such as Alcohol Use Disorder, have been shown to be comorbid with bipolar disorders, psychotic disorders, anxiety, and depression (American Psychiatric Association 2013). Further, it is estimated that when it comes to gambling disorder, 75 percent of males diagnosed with a gambling disorder would also meet criteria for an alcohol use disorder (Barnhill 2018). In the past, individuals with multiple SUDs were diagnosed with polysubstance dependence whereas today each SUD is listed separately as its own diagnosis.

The American Psychiatric Association's (2013) diagnostic criteria for SUDs contrasts with the American Bar Association's (ABA) published symptoms on "drug use disorders."[2] The ABA's drug use disorders symptoms appear to correspond more to what would be referred to as a substance-induced disorder such as intoxication rather than a SUD. We find it perplexing as to why the ABA would come up with their own criteria; not only is this confusing but gives the wrong impression that the problem is less serious than it really is.

To highlight the chronic substance issues facing attorneys today, we focus on disciplinary cases indicating SUD and dependence. This chapter, broken up by substance, includes actual examples of attorneys who have introduced evidence of their substance use problems during their disciplinary hearings.

ALCOHOL USE DISORDER

Alcohol use disorder is diagnosed in individuals who meet criteria for a SUD through their consumption of alcohol. The disorder, characterized by behavioral and physiological symptoms, can take up a significant amount of time in an individual's life given the time spent procuring, consuming, and recovering from the effects of alcohol use (American Psychiatric Association, 2013). Alcohol use has been shown to affect systems and structures within the entire body and can over time lead to chronic problems involving neurocognitive impairment and other mental health conditions. Specifically, the disorder has been associated with mental health conditions such as depression, anxiety, and sleep problems (American Psychiatric Association, 2013).

As reported in the literature, alcohol is a highly used substance within the legal community. In our research, the term "alcohol" was the most frequently used term we found while searching for mental health and substance use disorders. Our results showed a total of 216 cases out of 9,942 attorney disciplinary opinions that mentioned alcohol. These cases represented just 2.2 percent of reported cases between 2010–2020 which was far lower than the prevalence rates found in the community and prior attorney research (see Table 4.1 for comparison). A select few are described in further detail below.

CASE EXAMPLE #21: *IOWA V. NELSON* (2013)

Criminal defense attorney Nelson started a solo practice after the firm he worked for dissolved. He shared an office with other attorneys and successfully grew his practice to about "anywhere from 100 to 120 [Operating While Intoxicated] OWIs a year" (*Nelson* 2013, 532).

But in 2009 Nelson began having marital problems that led to negative consequences. He left the home he shared with his wife on Thanksgiving Day and started "drinking pretty hard" (*Nelson* 2013, 532). Soon thereafter he and his wife split up. He let his practice "slip[. . .] through the cracks" (*Nelson* 2013, 532); he decreased his caseload to a handful of cases, left his practice, and moved back home with his parents. Around this time many of his client cases suffered as well. He failed to appear at court for hearings and pretrial conferences; failed to cure a default on an appeal; did not return client communications; and failed to send a client's substance use evaluation to the court. In addition, one of his colleagues who shared an office with Nelson filed a complaint with the state bar that

> …Nelson had been absent from the office for a number of weeks and did not keep regular office hours. His telephone and cellular voicemail system were full and had not been accepting new messages for weeks. Nelson had removed his computer and other equipment from his office. His unopened mail appeared to be excessive. Clients and court administration had not been able to contact Nelson. (*Nelson* 2013, 533–534)

The Board placed him on a temporary disability suspension in 2010 for abandoning his practice. At his disciplinary hearing the Board found Nelson had violated ethics rules involving diligence, communication, fees, safekeeping property, and termination. Regarding his violation of communication the Board said:

> Nelson neither initiated nor returned client phone calls, despite requests by clients that he do so. He did not respond to emails and calls from prosecutors and the courts. He did not notify clients of court dates, resulting in their failure to appear, the issuance of warrants, and subsequent arrests. He was inaccessible to clients who called while they were in jail due to the warrants. His voicemails were full for weeks so clients could not leave him messages. He did not open his mail. He abandoned his office, so clients were unable to make in-person visits. Clients resorted to leaving sticky notes in his office and, on one occasion, tracking him down at the local bar to try to obtain information about their cases. (*Nelson* 2013, 537–538)

In mitigation Nelson acknowledged his drinking problem. He reported he had since sobered up and had participated in several treatment programs including outpatient, detox, inpatient, and aftercare. He mentioned he also attended Alcoholics Anonymous. After considering an appropriate sanction given all the factors, the Board suspended Nelson for 30 days.

OUR VIEW

If anything, *Nelson* shows how easily a successful law practice can be upended by upsetting life events. Drinking can be triggered during acute periods of stress and can lead to chronic maladaptive patterns of coping which over time can turn into an alcohol use disorder. Here, Nelson did not present an expert to testify on his behalf about a SUD but he did offer his own testimony acknowledging he had an alcohol problem. He reports going through a cycle of treatment to care for initially what appears to be symptoms of intoxication and withdrawal (as evidenced by his statement he had attended a detox program). He may have benefited from reaching out to the Iowa LAP as part of his mitigation efforts.

An additional detail about Nelson's case is that aside from clients who had reported him, one of the attorneys in his office reported his misconduct to the state bar. It does not appear the colleague who reported him was part of the same law firm or in a supervisory role over Nelson because the court's opinion merely indicates the two shared office space, meaning the colleague may not have owed a duty to report Nelson's misconduct. The Rules of Professional Conduct suggest that the colleague did not necessarily have a duty to report Nelson but did so because he had reliable information that Nelson had committed an ethical violation that raised a substantial question as to Nelson's honesty, trustworthiness, or fitness to practice law. It is unknown if the colleague knew about the previous grievances filed by Nelson's clients but what is known is that peers who report misconduct can help impaired attorneys by bringing attention to potentially unconscious issues. Had the colleague's report been the only complaint filed, it could have served as an opportunity for Nelson to address his drinking problem before it worsened.

CASE EXAMPLE #22: *IOWA V. CLARITY* (2013)

Iowa attorney Clarity had practiced law without issue for over 30 years until 2009 when his sister passed away. In 2010 he reported struggling with alcoholism following his sister's death. At the time, he was handling several criminal and civil matters. In one of the criminal cases, Clarity charged a $75,000 retainer and transferred the funds to his firm account without providing an accounting or informing the clients. In three other cases involving Operating While Intoxicated (OWI) charges, Clarity failed to appear in court on behalf of his clients whom he had advised to not attend the hearings; all three of the defendants were issued bench warrants and jailed. In one of the civil cases he handled, Clarity failed to file a certificate and pay the filing fee on an appeal for summary judgment; his client's appeal was dismissed.

During his representation of these clients, Clarity sought help for his alcohol addiction. He attended a month-long inpatient treatment program in 2010 and again in 2011. The Iowa Supreme Court Attorney Disciplinary Board placed him on a disability suspension while he was being treated. At his disability suspension hearing he requested the Board reinstate his license by stating:

> I am asking the court to end this suspension so that I can go back to what I love doing. I have taken the necessary steps to put my life in order as would a

cancer patient, patient with MS or any other patient with a treatment of a disease. Alcoholism is chronic, progressive, and it's fatal. To that and in that there is no doubt. If I drink again, I will die. Simple. (*Clarity* 2013, 651)

The Board reinstated his license the day after the hearing in 2011 but placed him back on a disability suspension when he relapsed in 2012. The Board alleged he violated 10 ethical rules on the previously mentioned client cases by engaging in trust account violations, misrepresentations, failure to keep clients informed, failure to respond to clients' requests for information, neglect of client matters, and charging an unreasonable fee.

At his disciplinary hearing for the ethical violations Clarity argued his alcoholism was a mitigating factor. The Board acknowledged his treatment efforts which they described as resulting in "mixed success" but also stated he "has not demonstrated he has successfully rehabilitated himself to the point he is able to practice law at this time, and he remains under disability suspension" (*Clarity* 2013, 661). The Board weighed whether to offer mitigation and ultimately decided that Clarity's efforts to seek treatment warranted mitigation. Though Clarity was at the time on disability suspension status for more than 15 months, the Board decided to impose another year of suspension to "uphold public confidence in the justice system and maintain the reputation of the bar" (*Clarity* 2013, 663, quoting *Iowa v. Powell* 2013).

OUR VIEW

Clarity's case demonstrates how relapse can impact attorney work. It is unknown whether Clarity experienced problems with alcohol use in the past, but what we do know is that the court's opinion states he struggled with alcohol addiction shortly after his sister's death. As we know, grief and loss issues can easily trigger an increase in maladaptive coping patterns seen in drinking. It appears Clarity's drinking problems led him to neglect his client cases which resulted in missed hearings, bench warrants, jail time, and dismissed appeals. These client outcomes are particularly devastating and show the serious effects addiction can have for attorneys handling criminal matters.

In addition, Clarity's efforts to treat his alcohol problems were dismissed by the Board. Though he had attended multiple inpatient treatment programs, the Board interpreted his history of relapse post-treatment as "mixed results," as if to say relapse indicates treatment was a failure. Clearly, there were periods where his treatment was working. It is interesting Clarity compared himself to a cancer patient because the National Institute on Drug Abuse (NIDA) refers to addictions as "chronic medical illnesses" where "[i]f people stop following their medical treatment plan, they are likely to relapse" (NIDA

2020, 23). As an example, NIDA (2020) compares the 50–70 percent relapse rate seen in hypertensive and asthmatic patients to the 40–60 percent relapse rates seen in individuals diagnosed with SUDs. When relapse on substance use is looked at through this lens, it is perhaps more understandable to see that individuals with SUDS require continued, ongoing treatment.

CASE EXAMPLE # 23: *IN THE MATTER OF GUILLORY* (2015)

While he was a law student in 1999, Guillory drove himself and his cousin back home from a party. Guillory, who was under the influence at the time, crashed his vehicle into a disabled bus on the side of the road which killed his cousin. After failing a field sobriety test by police, his blood alcohol count (BAC) showed a result of 0.06 percent. He pleaded nolo contendere to a misdemeanor "wet reckless" violation. In his State Bar Committee admission examination, he "promised not to drink and drive again" and was admitted to the bar in 2001.

While working at the San Francisco District Attorney Guillory suffered several personal setbacks. His grandmother passed away, he got divorced, and he endured a difficult child custody dispute which drained his finances and emotional resilience. Also during his tenure as a county prosecutor where he prosecuted a range of criminal cases including DUIs, he was charged with and convicted of a total of three DUIs from 2008, 2010, and 2012. In his first DUI, the attorney was pulled over for not signaling while changing lanes. He was found to have a BAC of 0.18 percent at the time. He pleaded nolo contendere and was sentenced to two days in jail, three years' probation, and three months in the First Offender Program. As a condition of his probation, he was ordered "not to drive with any measurable amount of alcohol in his system" (*Guillory* 2015, 3). In his second DUI, Guillory was pulled over for speeding and weaving between lanes while talking on his cell phone. He told the arresting officer he was allowed to drive to and from work using his restricted driver's license when he was in fact not allowed to drive at all because his license was suspended. His BAC at the time of incident was 0.15 percent. He pleaded nolo contendere and was sentenced to 15 days in jail, three years' probation, and an 18-month Second Offender Program. In his third and final DUI before discipline, Guillory was found by a police officer passed out in his car with his foot on the brake while in traffic. He was difficult to wake up; when he came to, he was "disoriented," got out of the vehicle without putting it into park, and denied drinking at all (*Guillory* 2015, 4). He had a BAC of .24 percent and again pleaded nolo contendere to misdemeanor DUI. He was sentenced to 180 days of home detention, five years' probation, and ordered not to drink alcohol or enter bars. The attorney lost his job at the District Attorney office after his third DUI.

In spite of being involved in an alcohol-related accident and incurring three DUIs, the state bar found he "equivocated" at his disciplinary hearing about identifying himself as an alcoholic (*Guillory* 2015, 5). He participated in the State Bar's Lawyer Assistance Program (LAP) after his final DUI but tested positive for substances while in rehabilitation before dropping out of the program. The State Bar recommended disbarment after concluding that the attorney's multiple DUI offenses amounted to moral turpitude. They further noted that before each DUI offense he had attempted to avoid getting out of the violation by "[trying] to persuade the officers not to arrest him because he was a prosecutor. . ." (*Guillory* 2015, 4). The court said:

> We are troubled by [his] repeated attempts to leverage his position as a criminal prosecutor to avoid arrest and his lies to the officers about his alcohol consumption. He incorrectly characterizes this behavior as typical conduct for a person facing arrest. In fact, [his] persistent efforts to exploit his insider status as an attorney in the criminal justice system demonstrate a disturbing lack of respect for the integrity of the legal system and the profession. (*Guillory* 2015, 7–8)

OUR VIEW

As we know about alcohol and drug dependence, it can be a debilitating disease where individuals go to great lengths to conceal their behaviors out of shame, fear, or denial. In Guillory's case, it appears the efforts he made possibly went even further as he had to reconcile the difference between his behaviors and his identities as a prosecutor, husband, and father.

It is troubling to see the court interpret the effects of a serious alcohol dependence as moral turpitude and grounds for disbarment. Alcohol dependence is a serious and potentially life-threatening medical condition that requires treatment. Equating alcoholism to moral turpitude, which the California Supreme Court defined as "a deficiency in any character trait necessary for the practice of law (such as trustworthiness, honesty, fairness, candor, and fidelity to fiduciary duties)" (*Guillory* 2015, 7) may reinforce the stigma surrounding attorney disclosure of a SUD and inhibit attorneys from seeking help.

In comparison, in two cases from Indiana, *In the Matter of Piatt* (2020) and *In the Matter of Broderick* (2020), the attorneys in each of those cases were arrested five times for alcohol-related offenses and received relatively short suspensions. Piatt received a 180-day suspension with 90 days served and the remaining days stayed. Broderick, in what appeared to be his fourth offense, had a .29 percent BAC after leaving the scene of a vehicle accident and was handed down a one-year suspension. Of course, cases from different jurisdictions tend to be handled quite differently with disparate outcomes but the inconsistency in which courts and Disciplinary Boards dispense with attorney discipline can be dizzying. What may be grounds for disbarment in a seemingly harsher discipline culture such as California may be a basis for a mere suspension in another state such as Indiana. Without consistent guidelines and consequences, attorneys may find it difficult to navigate or predict the attorney disciplinary process.

CASE EXAMPLE #24: *BOARD V. WALLWEY* (2020)

On a Wednesday afternoon in December, defense attorney Wallwey who was representing a criminal defendant on a misdemeanor for harassment was inside the courtroom with her client waiting for trial to start. The prosecutor, in an attempt to negotiate a plea deal, walked over to Wallwey to speak with her about the case. While speaking to her he noticed she appeared "slow and sluggish, her eyes were very glossy, her words were somewhat slurred, she had a slight odor of alcohol and when she spoke to me her eyes did not seem to focus" (*Wallwey* 2020, 1). Wallwey was taken aside for further questioning before the trial commenced. She denied consuming any alcohol on the day of the trial despite demonstrating signs of intoxication. The officer who interviewed her noted she smelled of alcohol, "her eyes were bloodshot, and she was slow to answer questions" (*Wallwey* 2020, 1–2). Although she refused a breathalyzer and standard Horizontal Gaze Nystagmus test, she eventually agreed to testing which revealed a BAC of .209 percent. She was placed under arrest for public intoxication, and her client's trial was postponed.

After her arrest Wallwey reported making several changes in her life. For example, she stated she quit drinking and is sober. Other changes she implemented were seeking help through the state's lawyer assistance program, attending counseling, and reconnecting with family and friends. The Iowa Attorney Disciplinary Board encouraged her to continue seeking mental health treatment.

In their public reprimand letter, the Board offered additional observations they had used in determining her discipline. First, they characterized Wallwey's behavior as "uncooperative" when she was confronted about her substance use (*Wallwey* 2020, 2). Second, it was noted her client's trial was continued so new counsel could be appointed. The trial ultimately ended up being continued "several times" because of the COVID-19 pandemic (Wallwey 2020, 2).

OUR VIEW

Wallwey's case offers a vivid example of how an impaired attorney's behavior can directly impact a client. Her client's case on a misdemeanor was scheduled for trial but could not be completed because of her impairment. The client had to be reassigned new defense counsel, and their trial had to be rescheduled, all of which likely resulted in an extraordinary cost to the client as well as the justice system. Wallwey was evidently impaired to others within the courtroom but not to herself. It is startling to think she arrived at the courthouse that day, went through security, and sat with her client all while under the influence.

One of the important points to remember in substance use cases, as compared with, for example, PTSD, anxiety, and depression, is that denial can be a powerful coping mechanism to delay facing the truth. In denial, a person may rationalize their use of alcohol and/or minimize the problem. Attorneys with substance use problems may even seem to be untruthful or dishonest in comparison with attorneys who present with other mental health disorders. It is quite common for individuals struggling with alcohol dependence issues to be unaware of the repercussions of their use. Thus, courts may be especially harsh on these respondents because they do not readily admit to their problems or seek treatment. Here, despite Wallwey's obvious intoxication to others, she seemed unaware of the effect her impairment had on others as well as herself, and because of her unrecognized and untreated problems with alcohol use, the Board publicly reprimanded her.

CASE EXAMPLE #25: *IOWA V. STEINBACH* (2020)

Iowa attorney Steinbach was publicly reprimanded for what the Iowa Attorney Disciplinary Board referred to as "a downward alcohol abuse spiral." In addition to two arrests for Operating While Intoxicated (OWI) and one arrest for Public Intoxication, Steinbach showed impairment in her work as a law clerk at Iowa's Third Judicial District. Chief Judge Hoffmeyer described several instances of work problems in his report to the state Disciplinary Board:

June 6, 2019 – [Steinbach] was found smelling of alcohol, slurred speech, sleeping (passed out) on a couch during work hours and arrangements were made for her to be taken home. [Steinbach] was placed on administrative leave the next day. An examination by a psychiatrist took place. She was found fit to return to work and reinstated.

July 17, 2019 – [Steinbach] was terminated from her employment with the judicial branch. . . . [Steinbach] was a smart and competent law clerk. Her work product was good. . . . I understand [Steinbach] did not request help from any of the employee assistance program. A stumbling block for us placing any conditions of employment or utilizing any of the employee assistance programs was her never acknowledging or admitting she needed help or asking for help. (*Steinbach* 2020, 6)

In her response to the board, Steinbach offered context and follow-up to her issues. She stated that leading up to the time of her impairment, she had taken a job as a law clerk in a town where she had limited social support. She was "isolated, fell into depression, and turned to alcohol when a relationship ended" (*Steinbach* 2020, 7). Since becoming aware of her problems, she reported making efforts to reach out for help. She began participating in a substance abuse treatment program, went to AA meetings, and met with a mental health clinician.

In their analysis, the Board found Steinbach had violated Iowa Rule of Professional Conduct (IRPC) 32:8.4(b) which states: "It is professional misconduct for a lawyer to commit a criminal act that reflects adversely on the lawyer's honesty, trustworthiness, or fitness as a lawyer in other respects." In the rule's comment section, the IRPC adds: "A pattern of repeated offenses, even ones of minor significance when considered separately, can indicate indifference to legal obligation." The Board's letter of public reproval to Steinbach appeared to refer to the rule's comment when they wrote that they "typically privately admonish[. . .] an attorney in connection with an isolated alcohol-related offense" but that in Steinbach's case a public reprimand was warranted given her "pattern of repeated misconduct" (Steinbach 2020, 4).

OUR VIEW

Steinbach's case is a stark reminder of the effects that addiction can have on a young attorney's career. For many attorneys starting out, clerking can be a precursor to more opportunities within the judicial system. Being reported for misconduct and disciplinary concerns early on while clerking jeopardizes a young attorney's chances at establishing a career. Here, Steinbach had no support in the town she was clerking in, had started a new job, and ended a relationship. Steinbach was, to say the least, in a vulnerable position as a new attorney clerking in a remote area at one of her first post-graduation positions. As such, she may have been more susceptible to engaging in misconduct based on the unique risk factors of her situation. Given her susceptibility, it may be relevant to note that some attachment-based theorists argue that disconnection from others can lead individuals to seek out attachments with substance (Flores 2004). In Steinbach's case we can see how alcohol use during this sensitive period of time may have taken the place of interpersonal connections and acted as a form of coping.

Though there are many factors to consider in this case, we wish to emphasize the feeling of helplessness that can occur with substance use. Leading up to Steinbach's termination at the court, the judge in his complaint expressed a sense of helplessness when he said that because she did not acknowledge or admit she needed help, her colleagues were essentially unable to render assistance. It is unknown how Steinbach felt during this period of time in her life, but it is possible, in addition to being unaware or unconscious of a drinking problem at the time, her lack of help-seeking may have been due to feeling helpless herself. Substance use treatment literature recognizes it is quite common for individuals with substance use issues to not ask for help. Difficulty seeking help can be caused by any number of issues including denial, pride, shame, fear, or overestimation of one's abilities. Sometimes it is not until the person recognizes they can receive help that they seek help.

STIMULANT USE DISORDER

Stimulant use disorder is diagnosed when an individual using a substance within the group of stimulants (amphetamines, cocaine, or other stimulant-type substances) meets criteria for a SUD. Usage patterns for stimulants can vary and can be episodic with two or more days between using, daily, or by binging which is defined as "continuous, high-dose use over hours or days" (American Psychiatric Association 2013, 565). Stimulants are commonly referred to as "uppers" for their high arousal effect and the use of these substances can induce a range of reactions including anxiety, paranoia, hallucinations, aggression, and isolation (American Psychiatric Association 2013). Boosts to self-confidence and temporary feelings of elation tend to immediately follow onset of stimulant use while depression symptoms and suicidal ideation may occur during periods of withdrawal (American Psychiatric Association 2013).

Attorneys with a stimulant use disorder may use stimulants to produce initial desirable effects such as confidence and euphoria as well as to help improve work performance. On the other end, attorneys in the midst of withdrawing from stimulants may experience increased irritability, depression, and hostility that may be noticeable to others working with the attorney.

Initially in our research, we found no attorney disciplinary cases containing the phrase "stimulant use disorder" or "stimulant," possibly due to other phrases or words being used in place of stimulant. We searched for specific stimulants, e.g., cocaine, methamphetamine—the more prevalent ones according to research—and found a combined total of 61 stimulant use disorder cases. The majority, 38 cases, pertained to cocaine while 23 cases were about methamphetamine. Some of the stimulant cases we found are described below.

CASE EXAMPLE #26: *DISCIPLINARY COUNSEL V. POZONSKY* (2018)

Aside from working attorneys, judges can also be affected by significant substance use problems. In 2018 the Pennsylvania Supreme Court disbarred a sitting judge who had presided over many drug-related cases in his 14-year tenure on the bench. The court noted the judge:

> exploited his position as a judge to steal powdered cocaine—an illegal controlled substance—that was the principal evidence in criminal or delinquency hearings held in his courtroom. Specifically, he ordered state troopers who had seized cocaine which was to be used in the criminal prosecutions or juvenile adjudications over which he was scheduled to preside, as well as a court employee—his law clerk—to bring that evidence to his courtroom, where he stored it in an evidence locker in his chambers. He then surreptitiously and regularly removed quantities of this illicit substance from that locker when courtroom staff was not present, smuggled it out of the courthouse, and used it at his home. Pozonsky attempted to conceal his thefts by substituting baking powder and other substances for the cocaine he had stolen and used. (*Pozonsky* 2018, 833)

In his disciplinary hearing, the judge:

> acknowledged that he had used cocaine recreationally since the 1980s, including during his prior service as a magisterial district judge and during his tenure on the bench of the Court of Common Pleas, but he denied that he ever took the bench or adjudicated cases while under the influence of cocaine. Pozonsky further denied that he was addicted to cocaine at the time he began stealing from the evidence locker. But he admitted that he knew that the theft constituted a crime.

> [He] related that he first sought treatment for his cocaine use [. . .]; that he ceased using any controlled substances [. . .]; and that he remained drug free as of the date of the disciplinary hearing. [He] additionally detailed his post-conviction community service activities, which included volunteering at a homeless shelter and various community drug abuse rehabilitation centers. [He] also testified that he was completing a nine-week program to become a certified rehabilitation specialist. (*Pozonsky* 2018, 834)

As part of his mitigating evidence, Pozonsky offered 68 character letters on his behalf from fellow attorneys, friends, coworkers, and community members in addition to introducing three letters from substance abuse counselors who had treated him. However, he "did not introduce any evidence, either via expert testimony or through the character letters" that showed a link between his behaviors and the misconduct (*Pozonsky* 2018, 835). The Board was unconvinced that the judge's cocaine addiction could ever be considered a mitigating factor with respect to disciplinary action[3] and criticized him for not offering a "causal connection between his addiction and his actions" (*Pozonsky* 2018, 835). Ponzonsky was disbarred.

OUR VIEW

This case represents a rare instance of judicial disbarment. To put it in perspective, severe judicial sanction does not appear to be as common as severe attorney sanctions. In a study conducted by Reuters (Berens and Schiffman 2020) researchers reviewed over 5,000 cases and found that 90 percent of judges researched remained on the bench after being disciplined. Because sanctions for judicial misconduct appear rare, when it does happen the cases seem to be for misconduct that is truly significant or out of the ordinary. *Pozonsky* is notable because the case involves a disbarred judge but there are other powerful factors including the sheer number of character witness letters presented. It appears the judge was a well-regarded member of the community he served and had even become a substance abuse counselor following his issues with cocaine.

The Pennsylvania Supreme Court in *Pozonsky* held the former judge to the same standard as attorneys in that Pozonsky needed to demonstrate a connection between his substance use and his misconduct. The Board specifically pointed to the lack of evidence submitted on Pozonsky's behalf despite his 68 character letters. It appears here the Board was looking for testimony that an expert would commonly testify to, e.g., whether the misconduct was caused by his disability. This is perplexing given that Pozonsky had three substance abuse counselors, two of whom had treated him, testify on his behalf. If anything, it would appear that Pozonsky presented a plethora of evidence with respect to his substance use. Perhaps what might have helped Pozonsky most would have been oral testimony and cross examination of a treating professional. Testimony in the form of letters may be adequate in some situations but when it comes to proving specific elements of mitigation for discipline, having a live witness could be critical.

CASE EXAMPLE #27: *OKLAHOMA BAR ASSOCIATION V. SODERSTROM* (2013)

In late 2012 Soderstrom pleaded guilty to felony unlawful possession of a controlled dangerous substance and was sentenced to eight years in prison. He was scheduled to participate in a county drug court program before completing his sentence. Following his conviction, the Professional Responsibility Tribunal (the PRT is Oklahoma's version of a hearing committee) suspended Soderstrom from the practice of law and scheduled a mitigation hearing to address his alleged ethical violation under Oklahoma Rules of Professional Conduct 8.4 for Misconduct. The next month after his sentencing, Soderstrom felt "depressed" (*Soderstrom* 2013, 160) and "stopped to see friends whom he thought were 'clean' but were smoking methamphetamine when he arrived. . . . [H]e thought about using and went so far as putting the pipe in his mouth but did not light it" (*Soderstrom* 2013, 159). He concluded that while inhaling "some of the loose methamphetamines had . . . gotten into [his] mouth" (*Soderstrom* 2013, 160). He later ended up testing positive for methamphetamine which constituted a violation of the drug court program requirements. Then while attending drug court in February 2013, he was found to be under the influence of non-prescribed Percocet and was subsequently jailed for five days.

The PRT recognized Soderstrom's struggle with addiction. In his communications with the PRT, Soderstrom described himself as an "addict" since 15 years of age when he began using methamphetamine in addition to alcohol, Oxycodone, and Ativan (*Soderstrom* 2013, 159). He reported his longest stretch of sobriety was a seven-year span from college to law school where he was able to maintain a 4.0 GPA during this time. Soderstrom told the PRT about his treatment progress since entering the drug court program which included exercising and attending three-to-five AA meetings each week.

Despite his efforts the Board elected to accept the PRT's recommendation that Soderstrom's license be suspended for two years. The Board offered:

> While we are mindful that Respondent is taking meaningful steps to address and resolve his addictions, his continued relapses while in the drug court program adversely impact on his fitness to practice law. His failure to strictly observe requirements imposed upon him personally by the drug court indicates he cannot be trusted to fulfill undertakings on behalf of clients. (*Soderstrom* 2013, 161)

The Board wrapped up their decision to suspend Soderstrom by mentioning they needed to see a "substantial period of sobriety and non-drug use . . . before this Court can trust Respondent" (*Soderstrom* 2013, 161).

OUR VIEW

This case highlights some of the potential ways relapse may jeopardize a mitigation strategy. The Board noted he had tested positive for methamphetamine and was discovered under the influence of a non-prescription opioid while participating in drug court. These two instances of relapse led the Board to conclude a two-year suspension was warranted to prevent him from potentially harming clients. Had Soderstrom not relapsed, it is impossible to say what might have happened but one could speculate he may have had a higher chance of receiving a better outcome.[4] It is unfortunate the Board interpreted his relapse to indicate he posed a potential harm to clients. Relapse does not necessarily mean treatment has failed; relapse "indicates that the person needs to speak with their doctor to resume treatment, modify it, or try another treatment" (National Institute on Drug Abuse 2020, 22).

In Soderstrom's case, it appears he was in the midst of dealing with a SUD and in need of treatment. There was no mention as to the nature of addiction he had (again we can only speculate that it may have been a Stimulant Use Disorder) nor did there appear to be any presentation of expert or character testimony, although it is possible his mitigation hearing contained more details than we are privy to in this opinion. Soderstrom mentioned treating his addiction issues through "outpatient" work (*Soderstrom* 2013, 160) and AA meetings after enrolling in the drug court program. He did not specify receiving any treatment in the past, so it is possible his enrollment in the drug court program may have been the first time he had ever formally addressed his substance use problems. Treatment for stimulant-related substance use issues consists of non-pharmacological therapy (National Institute on Drug Abuse 2020), meaning there are no medications to help individuals with addiction to stimulants. Thus, Soderstrom would have likely had to seek out some form of psychotherapy to address his stimulant use.

Treatment issues aside, it is possible Soderstrom may not have realized he had a problem with substances until this case. As he stated, he was sober and high-functioning throughout his undergraduate and law school years. He may have been under the impression, as is very common for people who use, that he was in control and able to control his use given his abilities. For some, an arrest and/or conviction in an otherwise exemplary career may indicate the presence of a SUD.

CASE EXAMPLE #28: *SUPREME COURT ATTORNEY DISCIPLINARY BOARD V. ROUSH* (2013)

Federal criminal defense attorney Roush was reported to the Iowa Complainant Board for an ethical violation stemming from a criminal offense. Leading up to his conviction, Roush engaged in "problematic" drinking, along with some marijuana use, that became a "gateway" to cocaine (*Roush* 2013, 713). He reported consuming more than five drinks during events such as happy-hour outings and while golfing or watching football. Roush's substance use factored in to his divorce from his wife, and he and his wife had some child custody issues over their daughter. *Roush* reported feeling depressed though he did not seek help at the time. He commented, "I don't believe [the depression] was ever a diagnosable condition" (*Roush* 2013, 719). Eventually, he began using crack cocaine; his use increased from initially every couple of months to every month which amounted to approximately $200 per use. He frequently smoked the substance with an acquaintance of one of his clients. He reported experiencing no negative effects on his practice or clients from cocaine use. He further clarified he was "never. . . intoxicated. . . while practicing law" because he used cocaine in the evening on weekends (*Roush* 2013, 713). However, in November 2011 Roush was involved in a sting operation and found to have two small baggies of cocaine. He was charged with felony possession of cocaine base. He subsequently self-reported the charge to the Board, reduced his caseload, and cooperated in the investigation.

At his disciplinary hearing Roush discussed his struggle with substance use. He admitted, "I would not have used crack cocaine if I had not been drinking" (*Roush* 2013, 714). Though he presented no mental health evidence, he testified to receiving treatment after his arrest through a chemical dependency program, which diagnosed him with alcohol dependence and substance abuse, and reported attending AA meetings. When asked about potential relapse on substances, Roush told the Board, "I'd rather put two holes in my head," which he later clarified was meant as a joke (*Roush* 2013, 715). He reiterated his substance use had no impact on his practice or clients when he stated, "I believe I have been competent and fit to practice law before, during, and after my arrest and prosecution" (*Roush* 2013, 715).

The hearing commission pointed to two issues in Roush's hearing testimony that were worrisome. First, the commission stated his responses to their relapse question "shows Respondent continues to grapple with significant mental health challenges, even if he has taken steps to address his substance abuse issues" (*Roush* 2013, 715). Second, the commission was concerned that Roush initially "denied any knowledge of the crack cocaine" during his arrest (*Roush* 2013, 715). The hearing commission recommended a six-month suspension for Roush's rule violation.

In weighing Roush's mitigating factors before issuing his discipline, the Board acknowledged he had presented testimony in mitigation of substance use as well as mental health issues. The Board overall was unpersuaded by either mitigating factor. Roush's substance use, they stated, would be given less mitigation weight due to his criminal conviction involving drugs. The Board did not allow any mitigation for his "general and conclusory" testimony of "undiagnosed and untreated" depression (*Roush* 2013, 719). Ultimately the Board decided to suspend Roush from practicing law for a total of 60 days.

OUR VIEW

Roush presents an interesting case for discussion. Here, it appears the attorney met criteria for multiple comorbid substance use disorders (at the time he was likely diagnosed using diagnostic criteria and titles from a previous version of the DSM) including what would now be referred to as stimulant use disorder. He may have also met criteria for a depressive disorder around the time of his alcohol use (depression is often comorbid with substance use), but it appears he dismissed this notion when he stated he did not believe it was "diagnosable," thereby prematurely ending any inquiry into that problem. He reported a precipitating factor to his drug use was problems at home with his family, namely his divorce and child custody issues. One common pattern seen in substance use behaviors is when negative affect triggers drinking and/ or using other substances. Based upon the years leading up to his criminal conviction it seems as if Roush struggled with mental health, alcohol, and drug problems for quite some time.

His statements to the Board that his drug use had no impact on his law practice or clients minimizes the insidious and painful realities of substance use. Though it was stated he was often smoking crack cocaine with a client's acquaintance, it seems Roush was able to deny or repress any knowledge of a connection between his work and his drug use. As the Board stated when they connected the two, "Roush's criminal law practice led to the detection of his illicit drug use. . ." (*Roush* 2013, 719–720). In fact, the client who was aware of Roush's substance use tipped off authorities which led to the sting operation that ensnared him.[5] Clearly then, Roush's law practice was being affected if he had a client who reported him, and this in turn raises questions as to his defensiveness. It is seldom a positive point when the Board is left to wonder about the motives behind an attorney's behavior for the simple fact that Board members, like many human beings, may project their own thoughts and feelings onto the attorney. Thus, it is recommended that attorneys involved in misconduct truthfully speak to their internal processes when addressing the Board. Unfortunately, as it appears in this case, when the underlying referral for misconduct involves drugs, Board members may be prone to thinking the worst; that the attorney is dishonest, lying, or intentionally misguiding the panel when instead they could be engaged in a wholly unconscious and unaware process where their actions are more about self-preservation than deception.

Another area of concern Roush presented was when he offered testimony in the form of a "joke." Specifically, he replied he would "rather put a hole in my head" and "rather put two holes in my head" when asked about restarting marijuana and cocaine use, respectively. It is unclear how these replies landed in the hearing room when he said them but judging from the hearing commission's concerned response, Roush's comments alluded to suicide. Within the context of his testimony where he reported having (as the Board deemed) "undiagnosed and untreated" depression, any statement such as this would draw attention. For example, if a patient in treatment were to utter these words, it could prompt an emergent risk evaluation or at the very least would warrant further exploration into the meaning behind the statement. From a mental health perspective, testimony alluding to threats of self-harm during disciplinary proceedings should be addressed promptly and taken seriously.

SEDATIVE USE DISORDER

Sedatives include several sleep-inducing medications such as benzodiazepines ("benzos") and barbiturates that, similar to alcohol, act as depressants in sedating the individual (American Psychiatric Association 2013). The American Psychiatric Association (2013) noted there are two patterns of users; ones who started using sedatives in conjunction with other substances and ones who were initially prescribed the substance by a doctor to treat a condition. Misuse of sedatives can result in a sedative use disorder, although not everyone who misuses will become dependent, and tolerance can lead to increased doses of the sedating substance (American Psychiatric Association 2013). Older adults with a sedative use disorder have been known to experience cognitive issues (American Psychiatric Association 2013).

Sedative use in attorneys may manifest as significant impairment similar to that seen in individuals with alcohol use disorder. Absences from or neglect of work and poor performance on client cases or in court may occur. The attorney may be arrested for driving under the influence or suffer a car accident from being too impaired to drive. From a physical standpoint, attorneys using sedatives may be more accident-prone.

A small number of disciplinary cases in our sample indicated the attorney had a sedative use disorder. Below is an example of one attorney who experienced symptoms indicative of a possible sedative use disorder.

CASE EXAMPLE #29: *IN THE MATTER OF PETERS* (2018)

In 2017 California attorney Peters who worked as a university associate professor teaching business, employment, and labor law was recommended for disbarment stemming from problems associated with her chronic prescription use. After being confronted by her doctors for filling multiple prescriptions, she closed her practice and transferred her cases to another attorney. She said she thought she "could manage" herself and "just needed better willpower to deal with the issue" (*Peters* 2018, 3). She added, "I thought I was in control. But I clearly wasn't" (*Peters* 2018, 4).

In 2013 Peters crashed the vehicle she was driving. The other car involved, carrying a wife and husband, were seriously injured and the husband died as a result of the accident. Police discovered 124 pills in her purse which were from new prescriptions she had just filled. She initially stated she took two pills before later admitting she took six or seven pills. After doing some math, police figured she was missing a total of 11 pills which she was unable to account for. It was later discovered during the investigation she was under the influence of Cymbalta, Xanax, Wellbutrin, Restoril, Neurontin, Topril, Lisinopril, and Tramadol. While meeting with probation before her sentencing, Peters, who was noted to be "scared and nervous," denied being impaired at the time of the accident (*Peters* 2018, 7). She was convicted of vehicular manslaughter without gross negligence, sentenced to 364 days in jail, five years of probation, and 18 months of DUI classes.

The hearing judge and state bar trial counsel recommended disbarment based on moral turpitude. Though Peters argued against that characterization and sanction by stating she "did not know she was addicted. . . nor did she feel impaired the day of the collision" (8), the State Bar Court determined she had committed an act of moral turpitude by telling police she had two pills instead of the actual dose she had taken. The court also found she did not accurately report her prescription use to her probation officer when she denied being impaired. She was offered no mitigation for her prescription use and was disbarred.

OUR VIEW

Peters is a tragic case that follows a familiar pattern seen in sedative use disorder. As you may remember, the effects of sedative misuse can mimic alcohol use in its impairment; individuals using sedatives can experience problems at work and are at increased risk for accidents. Here, Peters closed down her practice and transferred her clients after being confronted by her doctor on her prescription use which seems to indicate she was aware of her misuse and attempted to prevent any further negative effect on her work. Like many individuals who struggle with substance use issues, she may have presumed she had taken care of the problem when she shut down her practice; indeed, she indicated a sense of denial in her statements afterwards where she said she thought she could manage herself and just needed more willpower.[6]

Chronic substance use, however, is not about willpower. The prevailing model of substance use in the recovery community is the biopsychosocial model that views addiction as a combination of "biological, genetic, personality, psychological, cognitive, social, cultural, and environmental factors" that necessitates a holistic evaluation of the individual (Skewes and Gonzalez 2013, 62). The biopsychosocial model therefore takes into account many more factors that contribute to substance use, none of which rely on any single factor or are based on willpower.

Another issue we find noteworthy with respect to Peters' substance use is the state bar court's interpretation of moral turpitude. Moral turpitude, if you may recall from *In the Matter of Guillory* (2015), can refer to a character deficiency, "such a serious breach of a duty owed," or "such a flagrant disrespect for the law" that the behavior erodes the public's perception of the legal field (*Peters* 2018, 9). In this example the California State Bar Court pointed to "deficiencies" in Peters' character over her statements about her prescription pill use to custody officers, her criminal conviction stemming from the car accident, and her denial of impairment following the accident as proof of moral turpitude. In what appears to be an effort to convince Peters she had to have known about her serious issues with sedative use, the court wrote:

> ...she did not feel impaired the day of the collision. But, in fact, she was significantly impaired, as shown by her conviction for vehicular manslaughter while intoxicated, her wildly erratic driving, her failure to apply the brakes, and, after the collision, her physical appearance, lack of balance, difficulty following instructions, and inability to pass multiple SFSTs. Whether she perceived that she was impaired, she knew or should have known that it was unsafe and unlawful to drive after taking more than a full day's dose of Neurontin in five hours. She had been taking the drug for years, had felt sedated by it before, and knew or should have known about its common side effects of dizziness, sedation, and

lack of muscle control. Peters should have stopped driving after she breached the curb, yet she did not. (*Peters* 2018, 10)

The court's reasoning, however, fails to take into account the nature of chronic substance use, and more specifically, sedative use. The court infers an awareness on Peters' end that she knew of the effects her substance use had on her and could have on others and that in spite of this knowledge she continued. Though this assumption has borne out unproven time after time, the court imputes a substantial responsibility of self-awareness on Peters, one in which we do not believe is wholly achievable for most individuals struggling with recovery. Here, the court's admonition of Peters' behavior feels more condemning or punitive than curative and bolsters the perception that attorneys with chronic substance use issues are undeserving of mitigation.

CASE EXAMPLE #30: *IN RE JORDAN* (2017)

Jordan had been a member of the South Carolina Bar since 1983. Between 1999 and 2005, Jordan was found to have mismanaged 15 client trust accounts and their records. In some of the cases, he paid himself or the firm more than what was owed in fees but in other cases he paid others more than the share they were due. At his panel hearing in 2011, he introduced affidavits from two of his physicians of a substance use disorder history as well as a lymphoma diagnosis. He further reported having a "debilitating mental disorder" although no further description is provided regarding this fact (*Jordan* 2017, 608). Jordan's physician stated that the attorney was "addicted to benzodiazepines" up until 2004 and that his addiction resulted in "long-term cognitive effects, including memory loss" which impacted his work (*Jordan* 2017, 619–620). Jordan and the hearing panel agreed to a public reprimand on the charges based on there being a lack of evidence indicating dishonesty. The hearing panel offered, "While there was a pattern of accounting errors made by [Mr. Jordan], none amounted to dishonest or fraudulent conduct" (*Jordan* 2017, 598). Before his case could be finalized, a second set of complaints involving mismanagement of fees between 2009–2012 were alleged against Jordan by another attorney. The second set of grievances, which the Disciplinary Board described as "more serious" than the first, involved fee issues across seven client matters (*Jordan* 2017, 597).

The South Carolina Supreme Court combined the two sets of Jordan's misconduct charges into one decision recommending disbarment. In all, the Board found he had violated several rules including competence, fees, and conflict of interest among others. The Board determined he did not satisfy the requirements for chemical dependency mitigation under ABA Standard

9.32(i)(4) because he did not prove that the behaviors which led to his misconduct stopped after he ceased misusing benzodiazepines. Though the Board acknowledged they were aware of Jordan's substance use and medical problems, they stated ". . . the timing of Jordan's misconduct in the second set of charges undermines his [mitigation] arguments" in part because his misconduct continued "well after he overcame his prescription drug problems" in 2004 (*Jordan* 2017, 620). The Board went on to express a feeling of consternation over why Jordan incurred the second set of complaints. The Board stated:

> It makes no sense that a person of Mr. Jordan's intelligence and experience could "accidentally" fail to pay his co-counsel, then—while under investigation by Disciplinary Counsel for doing so—continue to accidentally do the same thing. As the panel noted in its report on the second set of charges, "Even if we were to give [Mr. Jordan] the benefit of the doubt and attribute his repeated misrepresentations to [the referring attorney] to inadvertence or poor recollection, it defies logic that he would be so careless given the serious nature of the disciplinary proceedings pending against him at the time." . . . The second set of charges. . . leave no room for any finding other than intentional misconduct (*Jordan* 2017, 620–621).

OUR VIEW

We agree that Jordan's conduct "defies logic" and necessitates further inquiry but disagree about there being no room for alternative explanations. As he presented to the hearing panel, Jordan struggled with both sedative dependence and cancer. One can only imagine the impact these health issues had on him personally. Professionally, it appears his health problems wreaked havoc on his law practice which had been in its 16th year by the time his misconduct began. The tragedy of Jordan's case is that the hearing panel had found no dishonest motive in his first set of complaints and recommended a public reprimand for his misconduct. It was not until the second set of complaints that came in while the first set were pending that the Board decided to disbar Jordan. Essentially, "but for" the timing of the new alleged ethical violations, Jordan may have received a different judgment.

Because timing appears to be an issue the Board pointed to in this case, we want to turn to the timeline of events. According to Jordan, he struggled with sedative dependence between 1997 and 2004, around the time of his first set of misconduct allegations which occurred between 1999 and 2005. It appears Jordan's mitigating evidence, e.g., showing he struggled with sedatives around the time of the allegations, was enough to explain his misconduct. In other words, the timeline matches up. But when he "overcame his addiction" in 2004, five years before his second set of misconduct complaints (2009–2012), the Board, despite receiving evidence from two of Jordan's physicians describing long-term effects of sedative dependence (notwithstanding the cancer diagnosis), determined his mitigating evidence no longer applied. It appears the Board rejected Jordan's evidence of continuing health problems in favor of finding "intentional misconduct."

From our perspective this is akin to calling a patient a malingerer. Malingering, or intentionally misrepresenting one's health status for personal gain, is usually considered a diagnosis of exclusion, meaning that other conditions must be ruled-out before arriving at a conclusion the patient has malingered. Malingering is known to occur more often in medico-legal settings where the patient is motivated to avoid some type of penalty (American Psychiatric Association 2013). Here, although it is possible one could argue Jordan (and his physicians) were malingering, the Board shows little proof of such a disturbing allegation. Other than having difficulty matching up a timeline of substance use to the second set of complaints, there does not appear to be solid evidence to rebut Jordan's health problems. Had the Board ordered Jordan to complete an independent medical evaluation, as does happen in routine civil and criminal trials, there would be a second opinion. For not addressing Jordan's submission of medical and mental health evidence, we are cautious as to the Board's conclusion of intentional misconduct.

We believe it is quite possible Jordan endured lasting effects of a SUD or even possibly continued using sedatives after he reported overcoming his addiction. After all, many SUDs have been known to produce long-term cognitive effects, e.g., long-term use of stimulants has been shown to result in unstable behavior, aggression, isolation, and sexual dysfunction; long-term use of MDMA has been shown to have damaging effects on the brain along with memory impairment; long-term use of inhalants increases risk for depression, anxiety, and many diseases including HIV/AIDS and tuberculosis (American Psychiatric Association 2013). Sedative use in particular has been associated with depression and suicidal ideation (American Psychiatric Association 2013); although it is unclear what "debilitating mental disorder" Jordan experienced, one wonders if it was a serious mental illness such as depression which would also seriously impact an attorney's work. The American Psychiatric Association (2013) also states that sedative use is correlated with other SUDs, so although Jordan reported he overcame his opioid dependence in 2004, it is unclear whether he may have suffered any relapses on sedatives or other drugs which could have contributed to his misconduct during the second set of allegations.

OPIOID USE DISORDER

Opioid Use Disorder is diagnosed when an individual who uses opioids (e.g., fentanyl, codeine, morphine, oxycodone, heroin, tramadol) for no medical purpose meets criteria for a SUD. Misuse of opioids can result in increasingly higher levels of tolerance that in turn make withdrawal symptoms unbearable for the individual which can lead to desperate attempts to obtain more of the substance. As such, opioids are frequently procured using illegal means (American Psychiatric Association 2013). Individuals who use opioids may present with mental health symptoms as a result of intoxication. The American Psychiatric Association (2013) states that only about 20–30 percent individuals with opiate use disorder maintain long-term sobriety.

Attorneys with an opiate use disorder may experience, as with other SUDs, decreases in work performance as a significant amount of time is spent procuring or using opioids and poor judgment. Additionally, attorneys who misuse opioids are prone to running afoul of the law themselves in order to obtain the substance. Just as healthcare workers with an opioid use disorder have been noted to steal opioids from their place of employment (American Psychiatric Association 2013), attorneys may take funds from clients or their law firms to fund their opioid dependence. These factors (e.g., work performance issues, time spent using or obtaining opioids, using illegal means to obtain opioids) in our view further increase an attorney's risk of misconduct.

A small number of disciplinary cases in our sample indicated the attorney had an opiate use disorder. Below are examples of disciplined attorneys who introduced evidence of an opiate use disorder.

CASE EXAMPLE #31: *LAWYER DISCIPLINARY BOARD V. SIDIROPOLIS* (2019)

Insurance law attorney Sidiropolis had been practicing out of West Virginia since 2007 when he was seriously injured in a car accident the following year. The accident caused painful "herniated discs with nerve root impingement" (*Sidiropolis* 2019, 780) that led to several methods of treatment including physical therapy, chiropractor sessions, steroid injections, and a prescription for Vicodin and Oxycodone. Sidiropolis stated the prescribed opioid medications he received were the most helpful at alleviating pain, and the drugs helped him perform his work. He used the drugs for about five or six years until he sought treatment for opioid addiction. He began a medication-assisted therapy program where he received Suboxone, a prescription medication to treat opioid dependence, but soon turned to purchasing the prescription "off the street" (*Sidiropolis* 2019, 781) and then later to using heroin as a cost-saving measure. The drugs, he stated, were initially used "to maintain . . . a baseline" of pain management but admitted he "spiraled" upon starting heroin (*Sidiropolis* 2019, 781). Throughout his opiate addiction issues, Sidiropolis continued to work until he was arrested, charged, and pleaded guilty to one count of a federal drug violation. He self-reported his conviction to West Virginia's Office of Disciplinary Counsel and was charged with one ethical violation of committing criminal acts in violation of federal and state law. The hearing panel recommended he be suspended for two years.

As part of his plea agreement on the federal conviction, Sidiropolis engaged in treatment through a Drug Court Program but also sought treatment opportunities outside of his formal requirements. He attended group and individual therapy, some of which was daily, and passed over 150 urinalysis tests (urine tests designed to detect the presence of drugs). He participated in the 12-step program Narcotics Anonymous where he became a sponsor for others and was noted to go "above and beyond" to assist his peers in their recovery efforts (*Sidiropolis* 2019, 783). Further, when he had notified the disciplinary counsel about his conviction, he had also reached out to his state Judicial and Lawyer Assistance Program (JLAP). For 18 months throughout his plea agreement, he complied with court monitoring requirements and went on to finish a six-month after-care program.

In considering appropriate sanctions, the Disciplinary Board along with the hearing panel subcommittee and ODC took into account the facts of his case. The Board found his three years of sobriety from heroin and completion of the federal Drug Court Program to be mitigating factors. Before they confirmed that a two-year suspension (a 60-day suspension with the remainder stayed) would "appropriately punish" the attorney (*Sidiropolis* 2019, 788), the Board stated they acknowledged his:

> . . .cooperation with the disciplinary authorities included his self-reporting, his admission that he engaged in illegal conduct, and his agreement to a variety of stipulations that relieved ODC of its burden of establishing clear and convincing proof of the same and shortened the ultimate duration of these disciplinary proceedings. (*Sidiropolis* 2019, 787)

OUR VIEW

Sidiropolis (2019) represents a unique example of how rehabilitation and recovery efforts after a serious conviction can aid a disciplinary case. Here, the attorney made significant strides to recover after falling into a dangerous addiction with opioids. As the Board noted in their opinion, Sidiropolis was cooperative with his disciplinary investigation. He not only provided the hearing panel with information about his case, he contacted the ODC first himself to report the conviction in a show of integrity. He was flexible and open to treatment through a variety of resources; he sought help through the state JLAP, requested to enroll in the federal Drug Court program, and became significantly involved in his local NA meetings. His three years of sobriety is remarkable and, as anyone who struggles with addiction knows, hard-earned. His efforts, combined with his abstinence, undoubtedly showed the Board he was in recovery. This can go a long way when trying to prove mitigation elements that speak to showing a period of rehabilitation.[7]

Of course, not everyone may have the same opportunities that Sidiropolis had. It appears he availed himself of every accessible resource which may not be feasible for others even if they find themselves in a similar position. He was able to participate in the Drug Court Program because it was made available to him as a result of his federal conviction, and he had to first apply for it and get accepted into it. He attended daily group therapy sessions and individual sessions (of an unknown frequency) which is a significant time commitment considering his NA and JLAP work. Even if he had completed the court monitoring requirements while continuing to work in insurance law during his stayed suspension, he would have had to juggle responsibilities which may not be possible for some attorneys. Thus, in addition to remaining open to treatment options, finding a good support system and becoming an expert in time management skills may help when faced with trying to accomplish multiple disciplinary obligations.

CASE EXAMPLE # 32: *IN RE ABDALLA* (2017)

Louisiana attorney Abdalla was reported to the Office of Disciplinary Counsel after he issued six unauthorized checks to himself from client trust accounts, failed to bill clients, and made fake invoices for work he had performed. In total, he took $39,085.86 from his former law firm. Abdalla stipulated to violating Louisiana Rules of Professional Conduct 8.4(a-c).[8] The Louisiana Attorney Disciplinary Board recognized two aggravating factors and five mitigating factors including personal or emotional problems. The court noted he had a "drug habit" of using oxycontin and misappropriated the law firm's funds to purchase the drug (*Abdalla* 2017, 1225). Abdalla sought treatment at a 90-day addiction rehabilitation center before entering into a five-year contract with the Louisiana Judges and Lawyer's Assistance Program (JLAP). He reported being sober since 2015 following his disciplinary complaints.

Abadalla pursued mitigation for chemical dependency under ABA Standard 9.32(i) and presented two witnesses who testified as to his substance use issues. The first witness, director of the JLAP, spoke about Abdalla's recovery status and involvement in the program. The second witness, the medical director for the rehabilitation center that Abdalla attended, testified about the attorney's "severe opioid addiction" and Adderall usage (*Abdalla* 2017, 1226). Abadalla's addiction, it was reported, began in 2012. It was noted that ". . . at the peak of his addiction, [Mr. Abdalla] was consuming shockingly high doses of opioids" (*Abdalla* 2017, 1227). He continued using for about another three years until he sought help. Overall, the medical director described Abdalla's recovery from opioid withdrawal as "successful" (*Abdalla* 2017, 1226).

Despite the evidence presented, the disciplinary committee elected to disbar Abdalla. The committee reasoned ". . . the thefts committed by Respondent, though done in the midst of a severe addiction, were executed knowingly, over an extended period of time, and with significant planning and forethought" (*Abdalla* 2017, 1227). Further, though Abdalla presented evidence he was affected by his dependency on oxycontin, which fulfilled the first element of ABA Standard 9.32(i), the committee did not find that he proved the second element which requires showing that his substance dependence caused his misconduct. They explicitly noted his experts did not present testimony which linked his addiction to his misconduct. The committee stated, "Though he may have used the money taken to support his addiction, that fact is not necessarily proof that the addiction caused his misconduct" (*Abdalla* 2017, 1228). Abdalla was disbarred from the Louisiana State Bar in 2014.

OUR VIEW

In Abdalla's case it appears the Board was looking for expert testimony to establish a nexus between his disability and the misconduct. In this case, though Abdalla presented two witnesses to testify as to his opioid dependence, the Board did not find his experts' testimony persuasive. The Board referenced another case, *In re Stoller* (2005), in which they stated, "Respondent's repeated and deliberate actions over this lengthy period of time belie his contention that his misconduct was an aberration." In other words, had Abdalla only misappropriated from his firm once or twice in a short span of time during his drug problems perhaps, his misconduct would be more forgivable. What this perspective fails to take into account, however, is the increasing levels of tolerance seen in opioid dependence that can lead individuals to engage in repeated misconduct over an extended period of time. As Abdalla's expert testified, Abdalla was using "shockingly high doses of opioids" as a result of his tolerance and likely needed more funds than he had to fuel this habit. We believe had he not been experiencing a "severe opioid addiction," he would not have engaged in the behaviors that led to his misconduct.

CASE EXAMPLE #33: *IN RE FOSSEDAL* (2017)

Family law attorney Fossedal was hired by a client to represent him in a divorce proceeding. Fossedal's law firm associate handled the matter until the dissolution was finalized in December 2009 and the client was awarded $117,225.17 in proceeds. The client's check was mailed the following month to Fossedal's law firm. Fossedal, without telling the client, endorsed and deposited his check into her trust account and made withdrawals over the course of the following year until the account was practically drained. After the client discovered that Fossedal had his money, he pursued her on his own and then later through a second attorney he hired to help him sue Fossedal. In 2012, the client filed a complaint against Fossedal with the board and won a default judgment totaling $161,186.75 which included the client's original owed proceeds, fees, and interest. In the end, however, the client received less than $4,000 in restitution. By July 2014, Fossedal had pleaded guilty to first-degree theft and was sentenced to nine months of electronic monitoring.

Over the course of a three-day disciplinary hearing, Fossedal presented evidence about her mental health through testimony. She testified to surviving three car accidents including one in 2006 where she experienced chronic pain ever since she was injured. Her primary care doctor prescribed her the following: Opana, fentanyl, Vicodin, gabapentin, and benzodiazepine. She denied experiencing any problems with addiction while on these prescriptions, and her doctor backed her up by telling the board, "[T]here's, you know, clearly an inappropriate lack of control and misuse potential but I didn't see it as drug-seeking behavior. . ." (*Fossedal* 2017, 229). On top of her chronic pain issues, she reported experiencing other setbacks; her grandparents died, she had marital issues with her husband, and had several health concerns. Others around her noticed she had changed significantly:

> She was lethargic, slept a lot, and was inactive even when awake. She would pass out midsentence and was unable to complete simple tasks. On the few occasions when Fossedal would leave home for a court appearance, she would need to start sleeping a couple days in advance in order to complete the hearing. (*Fossedal* 2017, 229)

Fossedal stated that the nature of her drug dependence led her to neglect the client's payment disbursement. She described herself as being in an "opioid haze" at the time of her conduct and could not recall much of the events surrounding the misappropriation (*Fossedal* 2017, 236). She attended a detox program for opioids in 2012 before beginning a medication-assisted treatment on Suboxone, an opioid substitute with less side effects.

The hearing officer determined Fossedal had violated five counts of misconduct surrounding the misappropriation of her client's funds and found a total of eight mitigating factors including physical disability, personal or emotional problems, and mental disability. The hearing officer weighed Fossedal's mitigating factors of physical disability and mental disability/chemical dependency to reduce her sentence from disbarment to suspension.

In a departure from the hearing officer's recommendation for suspension, the Disciplinary Board unanimously decided to disbar Fossedal. Specifically, the board disputed the hearing officer's finding that Fossedal met the causation element under ABA Standard 9.32(i)(2) that states "the chemical dependency or mental disability caused the misconduct." The board relied on stare decisis when stating that Fossedal's addiction to opioids, much like alcohol dependence, does not count as an "extraordinary mitigating factor" (*Fossedal* 2017, 232). Therefore, the board reasoned, disbarment was a more appropriate sanction for Fossedal, and she was disbarred.

OUR VIEW

Once again, in Fossedal's case it appears that the attorney's personal or emotional problems and mental disability hold little weight in the board's decision. Similar to *Abdalla*, the Board in *Fossedal* did not find she met her burden in proving that her disability caused her misconduct. Fossedal's primary care doctor testified as to her level of functioning and prescription use but, along with her, denied that she was misusing the drugs. It does not appear she was diagnosed with a SUD such as opiate use disorder despite the significant amount of evidence indicating that condition. This may have been confusing for the Board who, after hearing Fossedal testify as to her "opioid haze," had to determine what impact her reported physical and mental health conditions may have had on her law practice. Had Fossedal presented consistent evidence stating she had a SUD and that her condition caused the behaviors leading to her misconduct, there may have been a different outcome.

As we mentioned in previous SUD cases, there could be many reasons why the Board rejects attorney mitigation evidence. One explanation in particular is that attorneys may feel ashamed, embarrassed, or even humiliated during a disciplinary proceeding where they must present mitigating evidence such as alcohol or drug dependence. These negative feelings may be unbearable and cause the attorney to unconsciously suppress evidence that could help them in their case. Here, of course, there is no evidence in the Washington Supreme Court's opinion to indicate that Fossedal experienced negative effect surrounding her case[9] but as mental health professionals it is something we wonder about given the public nature and devastating consequences of attorney disciplinary proceedings.

NOTES

1. E.g., *The Addicted Lawyer* by Brian Cuban; *Girl Walks Out of a Bar* by Lisa F. Smith; *A Lawyers Guide to Healing* by Don Carroll.

2. "Bloodshot eyes or pupils that are larger or smaller than usual; changes in appetite or sleep patterns; sudden weight loss or weight gain; deterioration of physical appearance and personal grooming habits; unusual smells on breath, body, or clothing; tremors, slurred speech, or impaired coordination; drop in attendance and performance at work or school; unexplained need for money or financial problems; engaging in secretive or suspicious behaviors; sudden change in friends, favorite hangouts, and hobbies; frequently getting into trouble (fights, accidents, illegal activities); unexplained change in personality or attitude; sudden mood swings, irritability, or angry outbursts; periods of unusual hyperactivity, agitation, or giddiness; lack of motivation; appears lethargic or 'spaced out'; appears fearful, anxious, or paranoid, with no reason" (Commission on Lawyer Assistance Programs 2020c).

3. This attitude recalls the early days of mitigation where judges tended to view substance use negatively. Former chief counsel of New York's Departmental Disciplinary Commission for the First Judicial District Hal Lieberman once said, "I have argued that rather than being a mitigating factor, drug use ought to be an aggravating factor in disciplinary violations" (Goldberg 1990, 50).

4. Judgment and criticism of another's recovery efforts is often effortless. Certainly it is easy to speculate that if he had refrained from relapse, Soderstrom could have possibly been able to obtain a lighter discipline, but whether this would have happened remains unknown.

5. Given his relatively out-in-the-open drug use around clients, we wonder if Roush may have unconsciously wished to be caught as a way of holding himself accountable.

6. Individuals who have internalized a "moral model" of substance use tend to view relapse as a moral failing where the "people who suffer from problems of addiction are responsible for both acquiring and solving the problem" (Skewes and Gonzalez 2013, 62).

7. See *Oklahoma Bar Association v. Soderstrom* (2013) as a comparison.

8. These are based on the Model Rules of Professional Conduct 8.4(a-c).

9. She reported feeling "horrible" regarding her misconduct (Fossedal 2017, 230).

Chapter 6

Co-Occurring Disorders in
Attorney Disciplinary Cases

Several of the cases we just presented discussed singular mental health or substance use issues; in reality, these disorders often co-occur with each other and with other mental illnesses. To further our discussion on how these conditions may impair attorneys, we want to turn to disciplinary actions where the attorney reported a combination of disorders, commonly referred to as comorbidities, concurrent disorders, or sometimes dual diagnosis. Comorbidities are defined as when "two disorders or illnesses occur in the same person, simultaneously or sequentially" (National Institute on Drug Abuse 2010). Co-occurring disorders are very common in mental health populations; depression, for example, often co-occurs with substance, anxiety, eating, and personality disorders. Patients diagnosed with PTSD are said to be 80 percent more likely to be diagnosed with another mental illness including substance use disorder; and up to 75 percent of patients with bipolar disorder have a comorbid anxiety disorder (American Psychiatric Association 2013).

Though co-occurring disorders are prevalent, they can nonetheless be especially difficult to detect and likewise complex to treat. Individuals can have a more obvious substance use disorder that obscures a relatively hidden problem with mood or anxiety and vice versa (Barnhill 2018). Problems with diagnostic clarity in co-occurring disorders can result in treatment delays. Treatment may end up focused more on specific individual components of the person's pathology (the presenting or chief problem) rather than deeper, underlying issues that are driving the overall clinical presentation. Co-occurring disorders may require additional time to complete treatment as well which can extend the number of sessions needed. Many factors surrounding co-occurring disorders can delay treatment and rehabilitation.

SUBSTANCE USE DISORDERS CO-OCCURRING
WITH MENTAL ILLNESSES

Below are some examples we came across in our sample that show how co-occurring disorders can manifest in attorneys.

CASE EXAMPLE #34: *IN RE WICKERSHAM* (2013)

In 2013 the Supreme Court of Washington suspended solo attorney Wickersham from practicing law for a period of three years. In their findings, the court noted that Wickersham, who had practiced law since 1989, represented two clients around the time of his misconduct.

In the first client case, Wickersham represented a client who had been charged with driving under the influence. Wickersham did not show up to the court hearing after filing a motion to suppress, and when he did show up on the rescheduled date, he was noted to be "agitated, sweating, fidgeting, pulled strange faces, including baring his teeth at observers, and engaged in 'shadow boxing' or 'karate moves.' He asked nonsensical questions and made rambling objections" (*Wickersham* 2013, 1239). After returning late from a court recess only to find out that the court had struck his motion to suppress he "laughed hysterically, very loudly and walked off laughing down the hallway" (*Wickersham* 2013, 1239). His odd behavior continued at subsequent court appearances, and prosecutors attempted to have him removed from cases. He left several paranoid messages on another attorney's voicemail describing how the government was plotting a conspiracy against him, which prompted that attorney to file a complaint with the board. Wickersham declined to show up to future court appearances due to the paranoid delusions he was experiencing. At one point Wickersham was escorted by police to a hospital for a psychiatric evaluation and was diagnosed with substance-induced psychosis. Despite the events throughout this case, Wickersham never withdrew. Eventually the client took matters into his own hands, represented himself in court, and pleaded guilty without Wickersham's assistance.

In the second case, Wickersham represented a defendant who had been charged with a felony. Similar to the first case, Wickersham demonstrated difficulty with keeping his court appearances, either missing them or calling ahead to inform the client he would not be showing up. In an abrupt manner he informed the client he was "definitely not going to be practicing law" any more, although he did not formally withdraw from the case or inform the court, which prompted the client to hire another attorney (*Wickersham*

2013, 1240). The new attorney filed a complaint with the state bar against Wickersham for his actions.

Around the time of these two client cases, Wickersham's bizarre behavior was also noted at home in his personal life. He reported that his service dog was killed and his office and/or home were burglarized. He decided to run away from his home with his 16-year-old son. The two "drove [through] eight states" and stopped along their journey to ditch their current car before purchasing a new vehicle (*Wickersham* 2013, 1241). During this time Wickersham did not contact his clients or work on their cases.

At his hearing with the Washington State Bar Association, several issues were noted. Wickersham did not hire counsel to represent him, and he, according to the hearing officer, exhibited "continued impairment" as evidenced by his "rambl[ing]" testimony, "trouble staying focused" during the proceeding, and repeated references to a conspiracy against him (*Wickersham* 2013, 1241). Wickersham argued to the hearing officer that mental disability should mitigate his case and testified that his misconduct was caused by a "temporary mental condition" (*Wickersham* 2013, 1246). In addition to the earlier stated substance-induced psychosis, he stated he had been diagnosed with multiple conditions including "mood disorder, posttraumatic stress disorder, and very likely major depressive disorder" (*Wickersham* 2013, 1249). He presented an expert in mental health who told the hearing officer the attorney was "improving dramatically" and "would be able to return to full functioning at some time in the fairly near future" (*Wickersham* 2013, 1250). The hearing officer found Wickersham had violated seven rules, one of which was later struck by the Disciplinary Board, including failure to attend court appearances, ending representation of clients without taking steps to ensure their interests were protected, failing to tell clients he had stopped practicing and would no longer represent them, inappropriate manner at court appearances, failure to withdraw, failure to competently represent the client, and unfitness to practice law.

The hearing officer and Disciplinary Board determined mental disability was not a mitigating factor in Wickersham's case. Although the board recognized Wickersham's mental health issues contributed to his misconduct, they argued he had not met one of the elements for mitigation under ABA Standard 9.32(i) which stated he must show a "sustained period of successful rehabilitation" and accordingly they affirmed the hearing officer's decision to reject Wickersham's mental disability mitigator. Instead, the board allowed for some mitigation under personal or emotional problems before suspending the attorney for three years from the practice of law.

OUR VIEW

Wickersham depicts how an acute mental health condition could look like in the courtroom. He disclosed having been diagnosed with concurrent disorders including substance-induced psychotic disorder, a mood disorder (he reported possible depression), and PTSD. The combination of mental health and substance use issues is what makes cases like these complicated and difficult to tease apart. Though we are not told what substance he may have been using, it appears to have had some activating effects, similar to a stimulant, resulting in increased paranoia, psychomotor agitation, disinhibition, and impulsivity. Another detail we are missing is the timing and duration of his substance use; typically, substance-induced disorders like psychosis are diagnosed when the individual experiences an acute onset of mental health symptoms such as auditory hallucinations or perceptual disturbances after using a drug which usually go away once the effect of the drug wears off. Wickersham could have been using a substance daily or almost daily at the time of his misconduct; if, however, his mental health symptoms persisted in the absence of his substance use this would change his diagnosis.

What we find concerning is that Wickersham, who was pro se at his hearing, was allowed to continue representing himself despite his obviously impaired presentation. There does not appear to have been an intervention on behalf of the hearing officer (or anyone else in the hearing for that matter) to stop Wickersham as he testified, and even worse, the hearing officer handed down multiple rule violations after the hearing. In terms of mental health, we question what capacity (or competence) Wickersham may have had to represent himself. As psychologists, we have seen patients who have presented similarly, and we have referred them for medical evaluations, psychotropic medication evaluations, and/or crisis referrals depending on how impaired the patient presents. It appears Wickersham was hospitalized at least once (when he received the substance-induced psychosis diagnosis); it is therefore conceivable to us that at other points during his period of misconduct, and possibly even at his hearing, that he may have been in need of further psychological evaluation and monitoring.

Another issue related to the hearing we wish to mention is the hearing officer declined to offer mitigation to Wickersham for a mental health disability, and the board affirmed this recommendation in their decision. There is an appalling irony in denying an individual mitigation for a mental disability while they are currently experiencing mental health issues. Despite his impairment, Wickersham had the insight and presence of mind to argue mitigation for his mental health issues, and we commend him for his ability to self-advocate even if the board did not readily see he met all of the elements for it (it might have behooved him to obtain representation to ensure all of the elements of mitigation were thoroughly addressed during his hearing).

Yet while he had some insight into his mental health symptoms, it appears Wickersham did not necessarily grasp what further steps he should have taken to minimize the effects of his impairment on his work. For example, he did not voluntarily withdraw from representing his clients during the time of his misconduct though he failed to appear on behalf of their cases and told one of them he was "definitely not going to be practicing law." Failing to appear or telling a client you will no longer be practicing is not enough to formally withdraw. Had Wickersham actually withdrawn, he might have lessened the impact on his clients which in turn could have possibly reduced his sanction. For Wickersham to withdraw, however, he would have had to have been aware of his impairment, the impact the impairment had on his clients, and the need to ethically withdraw. It does not appear Wickersham was fully cognizant of his duty to withdraw, or if he was aware, he did not properly withdraw. Lapses like these are understandable when faced with more salient mental health issues in the moment but can really be damaging when not managed properly.

CASE EXAMPLE #35: *STATE V. JORGENSON* (2019)

Jorgenson was licensed to practice law in both Nebraska and Illinois. He moved from Illinois to Nebraska in 2017. Around that time he was suspended by the Nebraska State Bar for failing to complete his 2016 required MCLE. The charges in this case primarily came about after *Jorgenson* continued to hold himself out as an active attorney and engage in the practice of law in Nebraska despite being suspended. At his hearing he testified that "his life was in disarray both personally and professionally" and he was having marriage problems and child custody issues (*Jorgenson* 2019, 758). He stated he was "severely depressed" and had been consuming "a lot" of alcohol (*Jorgenson* 2019, 758). He told the hearing officer:

> ...when I went to the evaluation, I was as honest as I'm being here, that, you know, I don't think I had ever admitted—I didn't think I had a drinking problem, you know? I mean, I—I've been, like, a daily drinker for a very long time, but never a lot, you know, I mean, until [these issues with my wife], and, and I didn't even really recognize it myself, but I started progressing—or drinking more and more, and, at some point, you know, I'm waking up and drinking and, and it still didn't occur to me that, I thought, like, well, this is how you can make the anxiety go away and—looking back, it's kind of a blur, it was obviously a problem. (*Jorgenson* 2019, 758)

He shared he had been evaluated for both substance use and mental health and was attending individual counseling sessions in addition to AA. Despite his evidence, the board determined Jorgenson was not entitled to mitigation for his depression or alcohol problems. The board reasoned:

> Jorgenson did not present any evidence beyond his own testimony that he had depression and alcohol abuse issues and that he participated in group meetings. There was no medical evidence presented that Jorgenson suffered from depression, and there was no evidence presented that the depression was a direct and substantial contributing cause of his misconduct and that its treatment would substantially reduce the risk of further misconduct. Similarly, Jorgenson did not present any supporting evidence to establish that his use of alcohol was a direct and substantial contributing cause of his misconduct and that he is participating in treatment and ceased abusing alcohol so as not to make it an issue going forward. (*Jorgenson* 2019, 761)

The Board agreed with the hearing officer's recommendation for disbarment and disbarred Jorgenson from the Nebraska State Bar.

OUR VIEW

In *Jorgenson*, the attorney was very candid about his personal struggles. He testified that his marital problems led him to drink more and develop a worsening problem with alcohol which he did not seem to realize until it was a more serious problem. Jorgenson reported one of the clues to his problematic drinking was finding that he was waking up and drinking. Needing what is referred to as an "eye-opener" upon waking is one indication a person has a problem with alcohol use (Ewing 1984). This pattern of gradually increasing substance use until it reaches a problematic tipping point is very common. It is as if we are only capable of seeing problems when they have become out of control or taken over our lives. Jorgenson, for his part, was fortunate in that he was able to identify he had a problem with alcohol and begin treatment for substance use and his underlying depression issues by attending counseling and AA. It was unfortunate, though, that he was denied mitigation primarily due to a lack of evidence. He testified in an honest and humbling manner regarding his depression, alcohol use, and treatment, yet the Board did not accept this as proof towards mitigation. This serves as a reminder that some hearing committees require evidence that goes beyond the attorney's testimony.

CASE EXAMPLE #36: *IN RE SILVA* (2011)

Silva was a partner at Holland & Knight's D.C. firm when he was found to have engaged in misconduct in connection to a commercial real estate case. Before construction could move forward, Silva was to negotiate and finalize an agreement for an easement between his client and neighboring property owners. At one point during the case, Silva misrepresented recording the easement to the client. When the client found out about the status of the easement and confronted Silva, the attorney admitted to his wrongdoing. Silva's firm incurred approximately $150,000 of expenses not including 50 hours of time spent by another partner to rectify the error and, after terminating Silva, the firm reported his conduct to the D.C.'s Board on Professional Responsibility.

In mitigation, Silva testified to having substance use issues and mental health disorders. Specifically, he reported in a letter to Bar Counsel he had been struggling with alcoholism, cocaine dependence, attention deficit disorder (ADD), and depression. He reported he was a "regular cocaine user" (*Silva* 2011, 932) for 10 years but had been sober since early 2006 (before the misconduct in this case), he drank daily but "not to excess" (*Silva* 2011, 934) and had completed substance abuse treatment programs. He provided some insight as to his internal thought process when telling the forensic psychiatrist who testified at his trial:

> I will let things go, push things off, procrastinate and then I lie. I put off the easement agreement. There was no rush. There was no urgency until the end. I lied to my boss . . . I would always get things done. In the past, if I lied, I would do the project within twenty-four hours. I might be late, but I always got things done. (*Silva* 2011, 936)

He appeared to recognize he had problems with telling the truth and wondered whether this issue might be tied to other psychological issues. He added, "[I needed] help, not just with cocaine addiction, but . . . with my veracity, with my narcissisms . . . I think that I can . . . manipulate people . . . and that is what led me to this . . . that I can pull this out of the hat. . . did it a thousand times" (*Silva* 2011, 936).

The Board noted several inconsistencies in Silva's accounts which undermined his mitigation efforts. He was using cocaine daily when he made partner in 1995 and his use continued throughout his employment at the firm. In fact, he reported cocaine improved his ability to concentrate on his work. It was noted that Silva apparently had spent "$20,000 to $30,000 of his 2005 bonus and his severance pay on cocaine" (*Silva* 2011, 933). Based on his testimony, the Board determined that Silva's use of cocaine did not appear to contribute to his misconduct. Likewise, the Board said his testimony regarding his alcohol use conflicted and thus the Board did not find he met his burden in proving he had an alcohol disorder. In a further blow, the Board did not consider his ADD or depression as mitigating either due to his lack of submitted evidence proving those conditions.[1] The Board recommended Silva be suspended for three years and ordered him to show he had recovered from cocaine addiction before being reinstated.

OUR VIEW

Silva presents an interesting case where a former law firm partner,[2] testifying on his own behalf, may have inadvertently sabotaged his own mitigation efforts by offering details that reveal signs of relapse. This can be seen in the instances where the court's opinion describes several of Silva's contradictory statements about his past substance use, history of treatment, and current attitudes towards cocaine. It is generally known in substance use treatment circles that dishonesty is an indication that a person has relapsed, and that would be one of our first thoughts after hearing the evidence presented in this case. There is no doubt that Silva made misrepresentations, which the Board used to prove the aggravating factor of dishonesty, but the court seems to treat these as examples as if they are building a case for impeachment rather than understanding underlying reasons for this behavior. This is not to say disciplinary boards and courts should delve into hidden meanings behind attorney testimony; rather, we merely want to point out there are many ways to interpret an individual's words.

Aside from signs of relapse, Silva's testimony also highlights the ambivalence many individuals who struggle with substance use have about treatment. Ambivalence can manifest in a number of ways including contradictory statements, which makes sense when the individual may be very against using drugs during one moment and then in the next feel a craving or urge to use again. Silva's struggle with himself is seen most readily in his testimony where he debates seeking help with cocaine use, truthfulness, and overconfidence or what he refers to as "narcissisms." His testimony suggests he has flashes of insight into his problems but grapples with motivation to address them. Looking from the outside at his situation, we can infer there would be ambivalence about his cocaine use especially when, according to him, his way of doing things worked well enough for years at the firm. Since making partner, it sounded as if he had essentially used cocaine throughout his entire career at the firm, which would probably make it all the more difficult for him to decide to stop. Silva's testimony also made it sound as if he used cocaine as a pick-me-up when he needed to get work done. It helped him to, as he said, concentrate, much like a cup of coffee would for someone else. It is this line of thinking that makes it so challenging for people who struggle with substance use because they are able to see benefits to using while being blind to the significant downsides.

CASE EXAMPLE #37: *CINCINNATI V. FERNANDEZ* (2018)

Ohio attorney Fernandez was hired by four clients to represent them in debt settlement and Chapter 7 bankruptcy matters in 2015. Although he was paid retainers, Fernandez was found to have performed little to no work on the cases. Fernandez also did not communicate with his clients when he was called and did not respond to inquiries by the Board of Professional Conduct after they received notice that his client trust account was overdrawn. In a stipulation, the Board found that Fernandez had violated many rules of professional conduct including diligence, communication, delivery of funds, and recordkeeping among others.

In mitigation Fernandez testified he had mental health and addiction issues which led him to seek help through the Ohio Lawyers Assistance Program ("OLAP"). His house was foreclosed on leading up to his misconduct, and he experienced "repeated bouts of homelessness." He further reported problems with gambling addiction. OLAP proposed he get "inpatient treatment" for his mental health issues, and when he did not, they noted that he "chose not to" (*Fernandez* 2018, 380). Because the Board could not corroborate Fernandez's testimony regarding mental health issues with a medical provider the Board refused to offer any additional mitigation on his case and suspended Fernandez indefinitely.

OUR VIEW

Fernandez provides an example of unexpected negative outcomes when seeking help. Here, it would appear that Fernandez acted responsibly by contacting OLAP for assistance. He was clearly in need based on his reports he had unstable housing arrangements and problems with mental health, addiction, and gambling issues. It appears, though, that instead of getting help from OLAP, they recommended a highly intensive form of treatment (inpatient) that, although likely would have been helpful, was unfeasible or impractical for Fernandez to complete.[3] We are not sure what could have helped him at the time he was experiencing problems; people with unstable housing face significant challenges which complicates treatment efforts. What we notice, however, is that in this case Fernandez did not appear to get help for his problems, and his inability to complete the recommendations OLAP handed down seemed to be used against him when he requested mitigation.

CASE EXAMPLE #38: *BUTLER COUNTY V. BLAUVELT* (2020)

In 2006 city prosecutor Blauvelt, licensed in Ohio since 1997, was found to be naked in the government building where the prosecutor's office was located. Blauvelt was removed from his position as city prosecutor following this incident. In 2018 Blauvelt was stopped by officers on two separate occasions, once due to an issue with a headlight and once after receiving a call from another driver. In both of these instances Blauvelt was found in his vehicle without clothes on. It was later revealed Blauvelt had a history of having driven his vehicle without clothes on at other times. He pleaded guilty to public indecency and reckless driving and was jailed, fined, and required to attend a driver's course.

The Butler County Bar Association initiated disciplinary proceedings against Blauvelt for his convictions. Blauvelt stipulated to the Disciplinary Board that he violated a professional conduct rule against engaging in misconduct that adversely reflects on his fitness to practice law.

At his hearing on aggravating and mitigating factors, three mental health professionals, two psychologists and one psychiatrist, testified. One psychologist evaluated Blauvelt for a sexual disorder and found he had initially only admitted to the 2018 public indecency incident (in other words, Blauvelt withheld sharing his previous incidents of nudity). The Board found Blauvelt's omissions to constitute a false statement which was an aggravating factor. In mitigation, he presented his two treating doctors along with the Board's evaluating doctor who testified as to Blauvelt's diagnoses for bipolar disorder and alcohol use as well as subsequent treatment with psychotherapy and medication. All three mental health professionals agreed Blauvelt's misconduct was caused by his mental health and substance use disorders. His treating clinicians reported that since beginning treatment for bipolar disorder in 2006, he has been capable of stabilizing for periods of time but has decompensated when using alcohol.[4] In addition to therapy and medication, Blauvelt reported he contracted with the state lawyer assistance program (OLAP) for monitoring and participated in Alcoholics Anonymous meetings. The Board determined he met the requirements for mitigation of a mental disorder and issued a stayed two year suspension.

OUR VIEW

After reviewing so many cases where attorneys' requests for mitigation were denied, it is satisfying to see a case where a disciplinary board allowed for mitigation. In piecing together how Blauvelt was able to pull off a positive outcome in this case, we offer some thoughts. First, Blauvelt was represented by counsel. We believe his representation made a difference in the case given the amount and quality of evidence submitted. Stipulating to facts and presenting multiple witnesses is, from our research, quite rare in these attorney cases and leads us to believe Blauvelt's counsel assisted him in this preparation. Counsel may have helped Blauvelt with setting up the evaluation by the Board-appointed expert, presenting two of his treating clinicians, and entering into a monitoring agreement with the lawyer assistance program. The fruits of Blauvelt and his counsel's combined efforts resulted in the attorney receiving several mitigating factors (e.g., no prior disciplinary record, cooperation, remorse, good character) in addition to mitigation for a mental disorder. If Blauvelt's case is an example of what is required to earn mitigation, it is a high standard to meet for anyone let alone individuals with mental health disorders.

Second, *Blauvelt* offers us a glimpse of a true dual diagnosis case, one in which both a mental illness disorder and a substance use disorder co-occur and produce a challenging presenting issue. It appears from his history that Blauvelt was diagnosed with and treated for bipolar disorder years before he received a diagnosis for alcohol use disorder. These two disorders are so highly comorbid that more than 50 percent of individuals with bipolar disorder also have an alcohol use disorder (American Psychiatric Association 2013). Based on his treating clinicians' testimony, it seems that when Blauvelt is medication-compliant and participating in therapy, he is a high-functioning individual capable of performing the demands of his job as an attorney. However, it is a different story when he becomes non-complaint.[5] As he reported in his proceeding, Blauvelt becomes less inhibited during drinking episodes and it appears he engages in public nudity during these times.[6] His alcohol use, when combined with symptoms of mania or depression, can lead to perilous outcomes. Thus, it is always a relief to hear that an individual who is managing two serious comorbid disorders has a plan to address their mental health needs.

NOTES

1. The forensic psychiatrist testified he did not believe Silva met criteria for a diagnosis of ADD and that Silva's depression was "situational."

2. Had Silva not cost his firm a significant amount of money to rectify the situation with the client, we wonder how long it would have taken for his substance use issue to come to light. We can imagine in some work settings where a valuable partner with a mental health and/or substance use problem is still able to perform their job, the attorney's problems may go undetected.

3. There are other ways Fernandez could have corroborated his testimony regarding his mental health and substance use issues aside from seeking inpatient treatment, but it does not appear other options were presented or explained to him.

4. He disclosed "binge drinking" (*Blauvert* 2020, 894).

5. In general, when individuals with bipolar disorder discontinue their medication, they will eventually destabilize and either enter a manic phase or depression, either of which may require hospitalization.

6. It is unclear from the case opinion but it is also possible he may have engaged in risky behaviors like public nudity in the past while manic and not under the influence of alcohol.

Chapter 7

General Trends in Attorney Disciplinary Cases

Sorting through disciplinary cases is no easy feat. There is much variation among jurisdictions with often little consistency or explanation as to how sanctions were determined. After reviewing thousands of disciplinary cases over a 10-year period and whittling the number down to a sample of 661 cases containing mental health and/or substance use issues, we found several general trends related to how attorneys presented evidence to disciplinary boards as well as how boards and committees reacted to such evidence. In this chapter we discuss the themes that emerged from our research.

MORE THAN HALF OF MITIGATION REQUESTS WERE REJECTED

Overall, we found at least some mitigation was offered to attorneys who presented with mental health or substance use in approximately 41 percent of the cases in our sample.

Table 7.1 Mitigation offered in reported U.S. attorney disciplinary cases where mental health or substances use evidence was presented, 2010–2020

Mental health or substance use disorder	Number of cases	Number of mitigated cases	Mitigation %
Sedatives	4	3	75 percent
Bipolar Disorder	29	19	65 percent
Posttraumatic Stress Disorder	33	14	50 percent
Depression	238	117	49 percent
Anxiety	71	35	49 percent
Opioids	9	4	44 percent
Alcohol	216	63	29 percent
Stimulants	61	16	26 percent

Total	661	271	*41 percent*

Cases involving sedative use had the highest rate of mitigation, but this may have been due to the limited number of reported cases with sedative use in our sample. Bipolar disorder had the second highest rate of mitigation, possibly due to disciplinary boards offering more leniency for serious and chronic mental illness disorders. Both depression and anxiety received mitigation about half of the time in the cases we surveyed while on the lower end of the mitigation spectrum, alcohol use was offered a reduction in sanctions less than a third of the time. We discuss more details surrounding mitigation rejection below.

NO CLEAR PATTERN WHEN ASSIGNING WEIGHT TO MITIGATING FACTORS

One of the more striking trends was the lack of a system when it came to assigning mitigation. Though many states followed the ABA's Model Rules for Lawyer Disciplinary Enforcement, it was clear through our research that the reasons for accepting or rejecting bids for mitigation were far more various and complex than what we could glean from the disciplinary opinions. Disciplinary boards oftentimes rejected mitigation for reasons that were unclear or unstated. In fact, a significant proportion of disciplinary cases in our sample, despite discussing mitigation, contained no indication whether they were offering it or not to the attorneys involved in the case. Cases that clearly stated they were offering mitigation were included in our data. Thus, it is possible that some cases in our sample were indeed offered mitigation but that we were unable to tell from the face of the opinion.

On top of the mystery surrounding which cases receive mitigation, there was an added question as to how mitigation was weighed. Many disciplinary boards like to assign "weight" to their mitigation factors meaning that one factor may be weighed heavily while another may be weighed less. Unfortunately, there was no easy way to understand the significance of the weight or how the weight factored into the overall balancing of aggravating and mitigating factors. Nor were there any numeric values assigned to indicate weight. In some cases, disciplinary boards noted when "aggravating factors outweighed mitigating factors"; in these instances, attorneys were more likely to receive a harsher sanction such as disbarment. So even if an attorney were offered mitigation for a mental health or substance use problem, this may not mean much based on the "weight" assigned or when viewed in light of aggravating factors.

A SIGNIFICANT NUMBER OF ATTORNEYS
REPRESENT THEMSELVES

There is an old saying in the law that goes, "A lawyer who represents himself has a fool for a client." Fool or not, our data revealed a significant number of attorneys (27 percent) chose to represent themselves throughout the grievance process, including during their disciplinary hearings where respondents are afforded the opportunity to present witnesses and evidence as well as testify on their own behalf. The number of attorneys who represented themselves was somewhat not surprising; after all, despite the quasi-criminal nature to these administrative proceedings respondents do not have a right to counsel meaning they either have to pay out of pocket for another attorney to represent them or must represent themselves. Hiring an attorney can be cost-prohibitive for individuals who have had their license to practice already restricted or encumbered, thereby limiting their income and ability to pay. Aside from the cost of representation, for some attorneys such as the ones we discussed in the case examples, lack of awareness into one's own functioning may prevent them from making the best choices on their behalf. Accordingly some attorneys who represented themselves may have underestimated the nature of the disciplinary process and the skillset required to be an effective advocate.

Unfortunately when attorneys represent themselves in such high-stakes cases such as pending disciplinary actions, there may be an increased chance of poor outcomes. In our sample, all of the attorneys who represented themselves were either suspended or disbarred. Although we can only speculate as to the reasons for such a high rate of discipline, it appears some *pro se* attorneys were unfamiliar with hearing panel procedures which negatively impacted their case outcome, failed to appear in court at all which resulted in their responses (or lack thereof) being deemed automatically admitted, or failed to cooperate with their state disciplinary board. Our research revealed the latter was a common theme for *pro se* litigants and was occasionally used against the attorney as an aggravating factor.[1] One point about lack of cooperation is that individuals who are too ill may not be able to comply with the demands of state bar investigations in a timely manner—functional impairment for a mental illness or substance use disorder, for instance, includes problems keeping up with obligations at work and could very well result in missed deadlines or neglected paperwork.

CRIMINAL ARRESTS OFTEN LEAD
TO DISCIPLINARY ACTION

For the most part, attorneys who had problems with alcohol or drug use had been arrested for an offense. As you may recall, experiencing legal problems is one of the criteria for a substance use disorder so it makes sense there would be a trend of arrests for alcohol or drug-related offenses. Attorneys tended to be arrested either for DUI/OWI or criminal possession of a substance. Out of the alcohol and drug cases we studied, criminal arrests occurred in 37.6 percent of the cases. Attorneys who showed evidence of alcohol and cocaine use had been arrested in 27 percent and 71 percent of the cases, respectively. Arrests in sedative use cases were the highest with every attorney having been arrested. Further, all of the attorneys who had been arrested were convicted of at least one of the pending charges.[2]

PRESENTING NO EVIDENCE OR
INCOMPLETE EVIDENCE

There were many issues with evidence presented in the disciplinary cases. Problems in presenting evidence ranged from a lack of evidence to presenting what we refer to as nonpreferred evidence. First, many attorneys, despite offering oral testimony as to their mental health or substance use condition, did not present corroborated evidence of mental health records showing diagnosis or treatment.[3] Neglecting to present such facts seems akin to conducting a trial where no evidence is presented and the court enters default summary judgment for the opposing side. In other words, oral testimony by the attorney is often not enough to persuade the court.[4]

Aside from a lack of evidence, attorneys often presented non-preferred evidence. Presenting nonpreferred evidence was observed in court opinions where attorneys offered written testimony in the form of letters instead of live witnesses. Hearing panels and disciplinary boards were sometimes persuaded by written evidence that did not allow for cross-examination but there was a preference for witnesses who could testify in the flesh. Offering live expert testimony in general seemed to bolster attorneys' mitigation requests as if the mental health or substance use conditions were more believable when it came from the mouth of another (as opposed to the attorney's own testimony). This is not to say that attorneys were always allowed mitigation when offering expert testimony but rather disciplinary boards found expert testimony persuasive overall.

Even with an in-person testifying expert, some evidence appeared partially presented. In *In re McMillin* (2017), for example, the attorney submitted evidence of mitigation for chemical dependency but his psychologist also testified to an additional diagnosis of depression (McMillin had co-occurring diagnoses of chemical dependency and depression) which the disciplinary board disregarded. The board asserted afterwards that the depression diagnosis would not have changed their mind. Although the board's decision may have been the same no matter what McMillin presented, it is unfortunate he failed to claim both diagnoses as the combination of the two can manifest in a unique way and present with more complex treatment issues than either one alone.

TREATMENT SHOULD BE SOUGHT IMMEDIATELY

After reviewing our sample of cases, it appeared disciplinary boards had a preference for attorneys who sought treatment for their issues right away. The timing of treatment appeared important as boards expressed an interest in seeing an immediate remedy to problems. For example, in *In re Cairns* (2016) the attorney called Delaware's lawyer assistance program (DeLap) the day after he was involved in an accident where he was found to be intoxicated behind the wheel. Cairns made arrangements to check into an inpatient facility for treatment of his substance use issues. Although the board said they would have preferred he had more time in recovery (his sobriety at that time was calculated from the date of his accident in September 2014 to his disciplinary hearing in January 2016), they allowed for mitigation in part due to his efforts in seeking treatment. In our view of this case and other cases where we have analyzed the timing of treatment, the earlier the attorney reaches out for help, the better chances they will receive mitigation.

Seeking treatment immediately is somewhat problematic, however, for several reasons. First, attorneys with substance use issues, just as with any individual in recovery, may not immediately recognize they have a problem (*Attorney Grievance Commission of Maryland v. Patton* 2013; *In re Vanderslice* 2015). As we have mentioned in several of the case examples, denial and lack of insight into one's issues is a salient factor when it comes to substance use problems. Second, attorneys who are at risk of discipline or have suffered impairments at work may not have the funds or resources to afford treatment (*Iowa Supreme Court Attorney Disciplinary Board v. Wengert* 2010). Individual therapy costs with private practitioners can be a significant expense. Even more so, for some attorneys who are recommended inpatient treatment for their serious mental illness or substance use issues, the cost of such treatment may be downright prohibitive. One last consideration as to why attorneys may not seek help right away is that some mental health problems such as depression may resolve on their own over time without a need for treatment (*Disciplinary Counsel v. Longino* 2011). That is, an attorney who may have experienced an acute mental health episode during the time of their misconduct that has since resolved may no longer be in need of treatment by the time of their disciplinary hearing, thus rendering recommendations for treatment somewhat unnecessary.

FAILURE TO APPEAR IN COURT MAY BE VIEWED NEGATIVELY

Not responding to or showing up at one's disciplinary proceeding certainly does not help and in some cases could actually hurt an attorney's efforts to obtain mitigation. Many cases we reviewed where the attorney failed to appear acknowledged a potential for mitigation had the attorney come to court. In *In re O'Leary* (2015) for instance, the board indicated it would have considered mitigation for O'Leary's apparent alcohol issues as he had multiple alcohol-related driving offenses but that because he had failed to show and present evidence at his hearing, the board could not offer any mitigation on this issue. Refusing to offer mitigation without evidence is a common approach.

Some disciplinary boards took on a different attitude. In a reciprocal disciplinary case out of New York the Disciplinary Review Board in *In Matter of Chambers* (2017) viewed the attorney's absence from his earlier New Jersey proceeding in a negative light. The Board stated:

> ...although the respondent was advised to appear before the Supreme Court of New Jersey to show cause why he should not be disbarred, he failed to appear or contact the New Jersey Supreme Court in any manner. The respondent's proffered excuses, namely, that he was either too depressed or lacked the necessary funds to retain counsel, are inadequate and do not explain why he did not try to submit pro se papers. . . or appear pro se before the New Jersey Supreme Court on the scheduled date. . . The only reasonable conclusion to draw is that the respondent's default in New Jersey was deliberate. (*In Matter of Chambers* 2017, 202)

Chambers ended up being disbarred by New York three years after he was disbarred in New Jersey. Using a tone that implied disdain, the *Chambers'* board rejected the explanations he had offered for his behavior during the proceedings. The board viewed his nonappearance three years prior as a calculated move on his part and rejected his report of depression and lack of resources as mere "excuses." Had Chambers appeared in court, we could only speculate as to what would have happened, but we wonder whether the board may have been more sympathetic towards him.

NO MITIGATION UNLESS ALL ELEMENTS OF THE BALANCING TEST ARE FULFILLED

One significant trend we saw in our sample was the lack of mitigation afforded to attorneys who failed to meet all elements of the relevant mitigation test. Many jurisdictions use the ABA's four-part test for mitigation which requires a showing that: (1) the attorney has a mental illness or chemical dependency issue; (2) the issue in question caused the misconduct; (3) the attorney is recovering; and (4) the misconduct is unlikely to reoccur. All elements must be satisfied for mitigation. Most of the cases that were presented for mitigation failed to meet one, sometimes two, of the elements and were therefore rejected by the disciplinary committee or relegated to a lesser mitigating factor.

The two most common mitigation test elements attorneys failed to prove were causation and likelihood of recurrence. In *In re Davis* (2012) the treating clinician offered no opinion on causation which the board said precluded them from considering her testimony about the attorney's condition. Precluding the clinician's testimony effectively precluded the board from allowing mitigation. Davis was instead offered partial mitigation due to emotional problems for his attempts at treatment. In *In re Abrams* (2011) the attorney failed to meet the fourth criteria for rehabilitation. The board stated:

> ....the record contains no evidence suggesting he has overcome [his] disorders. We do not doubt the sincerity of his efforts to seek treatment, but the absence of evidence of the success of Abrams' efforts at rehabilitation diminishes the weight of this alleged mitigator." (*Abrams* 2011, 172–173)

Likewise, in *State v. Switzer* (2010) the board found Switzer met the first two elements of Nebraska's *Thompson*[5] test but not the third element that required a showing that "treatment would substantially reduce the likelihood of future misconduct" (824). In part because Switzer's misconduct was not mitigated, the board elected to disbar him. Although we highlighted a few cases, they represent a significant number of cases that were denied mitigation for failing to meet all elements of a state's mitigation test and show how important it is for an attorney to prove each part.

Overall, we observed many instances where disciplinary boards do not understand and/or appreciate the symptoms and serious nature of the mental disorders with which attorneys present. What appears to be most persuasive to boards: documentation and testimony from expert witnesses and other witnesses who can attest to the attorney's behavior and symptoms. In addition, attorneys need to do a complete job of linking their alleged misconduct to the mental disorder. All cases illustrate the importance of corroboration, documentation, and the critical importance of seeking mental health treatment.

NOTES

1. The commentary of the ABA's (2020) Rule 9 in their Model Rules for Lawyer Disciplinary Enforcement states that, "All lawyers have an affirmative duty to cooperate." Lack of cooperation is also listed as one of the aggravating factors Disciplinary Boards are to consider when determining an appropriate sanction for an attorney.

2. This could be seen more as a function of the selection bias towards publishing such cases inherent in disciplinary court opinions than the attorneys themselves.

3. E.g., In the Matter of Lingwood (2019); Disciplinary Counsel v. Adelstein (2020); Iowa v. Cannon (2012), Supreme Court Attorney Disciplinary Board v. Roush (2013); Matter of Hanrahan (2011); Matter of Bolduc (2014); Matter of Goldstein (2014); People v. Ward (2017); or Matter of Norton (2018).

4. There were some unique cases where disciplinary boards afforded mitigation to attorneys without any additional submission of evidence, e.g., Iowa v. Bergmann (2020) and State v. Moisant (2019).

5. The Thompson test requires: (1) medical evidence that he or she is affected by depression, (2) that the depression was a direct and substantial contributing cause to the misconduct, and (3) that treatment of the depression will substantially reduce the risk of further misconduct (State v. Thompson 2002).

Chapter 8

Treatment and Recommendations

ATTORNEYS AS (NON)PATIENTS

If you were to Google what it is like to treat an attorney who is a patient, you would find numerous results offering information about healthcare attorneys, medical-malpractice, and patients' rights advocates to name a few. In other words, you would find results related to attorney representation of patients and not necessarily results offering insight into what attorneys are like as patients themselves. Google's complementary "searches related to" section which takes the original query and finds related subjects fares no better; results offer linked topics such as "How to get a malpractice attorney to take your case" and "How to sue a hospital without a lawyer." It is almost as if the word "attorney" is rarely used in conjunction with "patient" to mean a patient who happens to be an attorney (or an attorney who happens to be a patient). This implicit, mutually exclusive belief about attorney patients, however, does not seem to occur in other professional fields.

By comparison, for example, attempting the same search with the word "doctor," instead of attorney, yields far different results. Doctors as patients is a niche research field unto itself, inspiring countless news articles, empirical studies, and books. As a culture we are fascinated as to how doctors react to their own care and how they handle issues related to theirs as well as their loved ones' mortality. It is quite an interesting juxtaposition then to compare how we research doctors vs. attorneys. Perhaps a better analogy would be to compare how attorneys handle their own legal problems?

To return to the original question: how are attorneys as patients, and more specifically, as mental health patients? That is a difficult question to answer for a myriad of reasons. First, it is a problematic question in part because of the lack of available information on treating attorneys. There is a paucity in the literature about attorney patients despite growing literature showing significant impairments. Another point worth mentioning is that perhaps attorneys are not open to treatment in the same way other professionals might be because of the nature of the legal profession. Being a zealous advocate for clients is rooted in opposition, or, the antithesis of emotional intimacy. Attorneys are trained to distinguish their client's case from the facts of the other argument, to persuade the factfinder that their side, and their side alone, is the right one. In some ways lawyering can be thought of as an exercise in narcissistic distancing.

Similar to other professions that require an enhanced ability to cut off one's internal world,[1] lawyering relies heavily upon the capacity to dehumanize oneself by blunting subjective experiences to provide the best representation the client deserves. Thus, it is no wonder that literature on the ways in which attorneys are similar to psychopaths exists.[2] Over time, as we have noted, many attorneys learn to cope with significant psychological distress through numbing and dissociation by various means including alcohol and drugs. Unfortunately, emotional isolation and addiction are powerful defenses against seeking help.

Lastly, some attorneys may not seek treatment because of an aversion to self-reflection sometimes referred to as psychophobia. Psychophobia has been defined as "an intense conscious or unconscious fear of introspection that is manifested through a variety of rationalizations that negate any worth of uncovering unconscious meanings in one's thoughts and actions" (Rowe 2009, 79). In other words, fear of looking inwards itself may prevent attorneys from getting help. Some attorneys may fear the pain of acknowledging their problems while others may be afraid to experience a deep sense of shame over revealed flaws and fear incurring a damaged reputation if colleagues were to discover that they were seen by a "shrink." After all, being a patient means being vulnerable, and being vulnerable is not something attorneys are known for. As attorney and author of *Lawyer, Know Thyself* Susan Daicoff (2004) states, "Lawyers by nature tend not to be introspective" (14). There are probably many reasons for the fear of introspection, as with any individual who leads an unexamined life; being a therapy patient requires, to name a few traits, motivation to engage treatment, being open-minded, having an ability to form attachments, and being resilient (Blenkiron 1999; Truant 1999). Some attorneys may irrationally worry about opening themselves up to liability if their clients were to find out they sought treatment for an impairment during the time they were retained. By the time an attorney has built up the courage to ask for help, problems may have already piled up so high it could be overwhelming.

STIGMA AS A BARRIER TO TREATMENT

Adding insult to injury, stigma within the culture likely suppresses attorneys from seeking help. In the general population, only about half of all individuals (48 percent) seek help from a health professional when experiencing depression while more than a third did not talk to any health or alternative service professional[3] (Substance Abuse and Mental Health Services Administration 2014). Though there are no statistics on how many attorneys seek treatment, it is estimated to be far less than the public. This is especially concerning given the higher estimated prevalence rates of mental health illness and substance use problems within the attorney population[4] as well as research showing stigma indirectly contributes to attorney suicide by preventing individuals from seeking help (Jones 2015, 12).

Systemic or institutional stigma may play a role in preventing attorneys from engaging in mental health activities. Attorney culture is steeped in the capitalist notion of "billable hours," and law firms, like most businesses, focus on increasing productivity and generating revenue. The law firm business model encourages attorneys to work as much as they can, often leading employees to forgo personal health matters in the pursuit of making partner, landing a big project, or increasing their recognition within the firm. Attorneys who are "workaholics," which may in fact be an ego-syntonic mental health-related issue in itself, may thrive in such an environment while other attorneys may suffer.

Stigma has been shown to be a barrier to treatment in several cultures, and unfortunately it still appears to be a problem within the legal community. Some firms may manage their staff using potentially dangerous denial as Cho (2017) noted: "Let's pretend that mental-health issues can be cured by paying a high enough salary and bonuses." Quinn Emanuel partner Joseph Milowec (2018) who openly wrote a letter to peers about his struggles with depression and anxiety said:

> To say there is a "stigma" associated with discussing mental illness in the legal profession, where mental acumen directly correlates with your livelihood, is an understatement. For a long time I did not feel comfortable admitting this to my colleagues for fear of being perceived as incapable or unproductive. But it is my truth. It is an illness like any other illness and it deserves to be recognized and treated as such without fear of stigmatization.

Stigma may also prevent attorneys from sharing their struggles with others within the same firm where the desire to appear invulnerable to coworkers may outweigh the perceived benefits of seeking help. Big firms, for example, have been compared to the *Hunger Games* where "[s]ometimes the attorney you really need to watch out for is down the hall" (Thomas 2017). Law firms would be much healthier environments if, say, mental health issues were normalized as being equivalent to any other medical condition. Thomas (2017) added "[M]y mental health is more important than my physical health. Maybe my managing partner can do something about that. If you manage a law firm, maybe you should do something about that for the attorneys at your firm."

CONFIDENTIALITY AS A BARRIER TO TREATMENT

For some attorneys, stigma about mental health may be tied to a fear of a lack of confidentiality. Though privacy is enforced through various federal, state, and professional sources,[5] confidentiality has been hypothesized to be "the most important hurdle to getting lawyers to seek treatment" (Neal 2011, 739). Attorneys who are concerned that they will be found out and/or ostracized for seeking help may intentionally deny or underreport their problems to remain under the radar. The fear of retaliation can act as a form of oppressive concealment within attorney work practices and can be damaging to the profession, not to mention potentially life-threatening for the individual.

ADDITIONAL HURDLES TO TREATMENT

Further barriers to treatment exist when it comes to issues of cultural competence and intersectionality. For instance, it has been reported that female attorneys do not seek help for their problems (Butch 2009; Neal 2011; Wait-O'Brien 2009). It has been theorized women attorneys may seek help less often out of concern they will be viewed as less competitive in the workforce or not up to the task at hand. Female attorneys, especially those in male-dominated law firms, have likely already had to deal with misconceptions and projections about their abilities for years so it would be understandable if they would be hesitant to engage in treatment that could confirm a vulnerability (Scienco 2019).

TREATMENT

It can be very hard to know where to turn for help. You may need help with an emotional issue and not know who to call. Or, you may not realize you have an issue until you get into trouble. Impairment due to mental health issues or substance use can be subtle, and it's often difficult for us to see the changes within ourselves. Some general indicators that you may need help are drinking more than usual, getting lousy sleep, or people close to you saying you don't seem like yourself. There are, of course, many other ways we can manifest distress so it's important to seek help early on.

DO I HAVE A PROBLEM?

Although it was 1988 when Bloom and Wallinger said recognizing a problem is the most challenging part of addressing an issue, the same still holds true today. Problems with alcohol or drugs can be notoriously problematic to identify for attorneys. One former associate attorney illustrated how difficult it is to recognize a problem even when it may be obvious to others: "My drinking increased, both in frequency and quantity. There were more blackouts and horrible hangovers. Still, the idea of being an alcoholic never crossed my mind" (Also Inside, 2007).

As such, the first step in any successful treatment program is identifying a problem. If you are not sure if you have a problem, it can be quite helpful to do some research surrounding mental health issues before heading down to the therapist's office. The National Institute of Mental Health (NIH), Substance Abuse and Mental Health Services Administration (SAMHSA), and World Health Organization (WHO) websites offer a plethora of information on mental health topics and how to find help. If you are searching for attorney-related blogs and websites aimed at addressing mental health issues specifically within the attorney population, there are options.[6]

TREATMENT OPTIONS

Once an attorney has decided to get help, the next hurdle is to figure out what type of help would be most beneficial. Treatment is vital to any attorney experiencing healthcare issues. There are many treatment and referral programs aimed at assisting impaired attorneys before, during, and after discipline. Attorneys who seek treatment not only benefit from the immediate health benefits but also receive fewer complaints.[7] What follows are various treatment options available through legal organizations, employers, or by private means.

LAWYER ASSISTANCE PROGRAMS

Lawyer Assistance Programs (LAPs) are perhaps the first option for many attorneys who are looking for treatment.[8] LAPs are comprised of counselors who can assess and evaluate mental health and substance use problems. Despite being affiliated with state bars, LAPs are confidential and most operate independent of state bar investigations and proceedings. As evidenced by the trend in disciplinary cases criticizing attorneys for seeking help too late, it would behoove any attorney who recognizes or believes they have a problem to contact their state LAP as soon as possible for an evaluation. After the assessment, the LAP may recommend a course of treatment or referrals tailored to the attorney's specific problems. It is in the best interest of the attorney to follow-up on any referrals for further treatment. For attorneys needing proof of attendance for substance use treatment, LAPs can also provide documentation on behalf of the attorney to the state bar. Be aware that much like a court-ordered drug treatment program could report its attendees' absences, LAPs can also report attorneys who do not participate in mandated treatment as part of their reinstatement plan. As such, it is imperative that the attorney attend their LAP appointments to avoid negative attendance reports.

EMPLOYEE ASSISTANCE PROGRAMS

Employee Assistance Programs (EAPs) are short-term voluntary treatment programs offered through employers that can address a range of problems stemming from the workplace or personal matters. EAPs are often advertised in workplace common areas such as the break room or through HR. Although many employers utilize EAPs with estimates of 75 percent of U.S. businesses with 250–1,000 employees and 97 percent of businesses with 5,000 or more employees using an EAP, only about 5 percent of employees actually take advantage of the service (Chartier 2019). Of course, this figure represents all businesses so the number of attorneys who take advantage of their law firm's EAP may differ but it appears that generally few employees seek help through work resources. For attorneys who may fear issues with confidentiality, an EAP may trigger some paranoia because of its inherent connection to the workplace. Attorneys should, however, be aware, that much like LAPs, EAPs operate independently and are run by licensed professionals who are bound to the ethics of confidentiality.

INDIVIDUAL THERAPY

Individual therapy sessions are the cornerstone of mental health treatment. Psychologists, psychiatrists, social workers, and counselors[9] typically provide this type of treatment. Court may mandate therapy under certain disciplinary guidelines, but it appears from our research this is rare and that attorneys tend to voluntarily enter into therapy on their own. Similar to attorneys, some therapists may work solo in their own office or work in a group practice with other therapists who share the office space. Most likely, almost any individual who struggles with anxiety, depression, stress, grief, burnout, or addiction could benefit from seeing a professional. If you can afford to seek out someone to talk to in private practice without having to use insurance, that may be the quickest way to getting help because there are less administrative obstacles associated with paying out of pocket.[10] Another benefit to seeing a therapist in private practice is more flexibility in treatment; instead of being limited to weekly sessions or perhaps only a specific number of sessions, the therapist and attorney may tailor the treatment plan to allow for more frequent sessions or a longer course of treatment which could result in better treatment outcomes.

OTHER OPTIONS

There are other options for those looking outside of traditional psychotherapy. Group counseling is one choice where attorneys may be able to find targeted support for a specific problem, e.g., a group on depression, a group for sexual abuse survivors, an anger management group. Group availability varies depending on the attorney's geographical area and local therapists, although group counseling has expanded its presence online in light of COVID-19 protocols. Because the advent of the pandemic caused many therapists to move online, seeking treatment through virtual group counseling or online groups is now more accessible than ever before and here to stay (Bray 2021).

A second alternative treatment option to look at is self-help groups run by peers, i.e., nonprofessionals. Peer support groups include alcohol and substance use-focused groups such as AA or NA but also include other groups such as the Lawyers Depression Project which offers online meetings. Self-help groups offer local meetings which are free or no-cost. Self-help groups can supplement individual therapy sessions for a more comprehensive treatment plan. For more information on self-help groups, an extensive listing of available resources in each state is located in the Appendix (see appendix online).

Other Considerations and Strategies

Aside from getting help, attorneys who are functionally impaired due to mental health or substance use may want to take into account other considerations. For one, Model Rule 1.16(a)(2) Declining or Terminating Representation states that, in addition to refraining from taking on new clients, impaired attorneys should voluntarily withdraw from cases when their "mental condition materially impairs the lawyer's ability to represent the client." This rule applies to all attorneys regardless of work setting but may be more difficult to comply with for those practitioners who may not have the wherewithal to recognize their impairments or those who feel pressured to continue working for financial reasons, such as solos or small law firm employees. Attorneys who do comply with the rule will find there is no reporting requirement, meaning that notifying the state bar is unnecessary and that "no one would. . . know that the attorney has sought treatment" for an impairment (Klingen 2002, 172) which could be a benefit to those concerned about stigma and privacy.[11] From a disciplinary perspective, impaired attorneys who proactively take steps to withdraw from work could be looked upon more favorably when confronted by Disciplinary Boards as their actions show acknowledgement of an impairment, a willingness to remedy it, and a desire to protect the client from harm. It seems then in the best interest of the attorney to voluntarily withdraw when appropriate lest they wish to eschew ethical rules and take a chance on whether a Disciplinary Board may restrict their ability to practice law for months, years, or even permanently.

Impaired attorneys may also wish to consider going on inactive bar status (Klingen 2002). This means the attorney is ineligible to practice law during the time of inactivation. Similar to voluntary withdrawal, inactive bar status would require that an impaired attorney who is aware of their abilities (or lack thereof) be proactive about limiting their work. While the thought of voluntarily deactivating their bar license may be tough or even painful for some, it appears to be a far better alternative to being suspended or disbarred for violating ethical rules. Switching to inactive bar status may even have a perk in that it can serve as definitive proof to the disciplinary committee, should the attorney be referred for professional misconduct, that the impaired attorney took steps to refrain from the practice of law while at the same time notifying the public of their unavailability (Klingen 2002). Again, as with voluntary withdrawal from cases, going on inactive bar status could prevent an impaired attorney's healthcare records, stipulations, and court orders from being exposed to the public while they seek treatment.

NOTES

1. According to the Great British Psychopath Survey (Dutton 2013) the most psychopathic professions in the U.K. include CEO, media (television/radio), salesperson, surgeon, journalist, police officer, clergy, chef, and civil servant.

2. See Dutton's (2013) book *The Wisdom of Psychopaths* where he refers to lawyering as the "second most psychopathic profession"; Johnson's (2014) article "Are Lawyers All Raging Psychopaths?"; and Thomas's (2014) autobiography entitled Confessions of a Sociopath about a female law professor who describes how her psychopathic behaviors led to her termination from a top-tier law firm.

3. SAMHSA (2014) published data showing individuals with depression sought help from health professionals such as: general practitioner or family doctor (37.4 percent), other medical doctor (6.7 percent), psychiatrist or psychotherapist (20.3 percent), psychologist (16.3 percent), counselor (13.8 percent), social worker (6.5 percent), other mental health professional (4.4 percent), and nurse, occupational therapist or other health professional (3.8 percent). Participants in the study also reported seeking help from alternative service professionals such as: religious or spiritual advisors (11.3 percent) and herbalist, chiropractor, acupuncturist, or massage therapist (3.5 percent).

4. To bring greater awareness to attorney impairment, CoLAP campaigned against stigma in a video published under the title "Fear Not: Speaking Out to End Stigma."

5. Professional treatment under the care of a licensed provider is bound by the Health Insurance Portability and Accountability Act (HIPAA) of 1996, state board regulations, and ethical practice guidelines.

6. See Above the Law (in addition to legal news, Above the Law offers a number of articles under the categories Health/Wellness and BigLaw which focuses on mental health issues impacting attorneys); Commission on Lawyer Assistance Programs (CoLAP) (a division of the ABA offering support and resources on mental health and substance use); the Dave Nee Foundation (a nonprofit organization aimed at destigmatizing depression and suicide in the legal profession founded by Friends of Dave Nee, a 3L at Fordham University who died by suicide in 2005. The foundation offers information and programs on depression resources as well as funds research on the topic); Lawyer Depression Project (a legal support group facilitated by attorneys who openly share and discuss their struggles with a range of mental health issues. Their website offers several ways to interact with other members including a forum, chat, and meetings); Law.com (offers a special report edition entitled "Mind Over Matters" that looks at mental health issues across the legal profession. Some of the featured sections include news and features, expert commentary, personal stories, and podcasts); Lawyers with Depression (offers a website showcasing a blog, podcast, CLEs, and psychoeducation on lawyers with depression by attorney Dan Lukasik who was one of the first to start a weekly support group for attorneys with depression); the People's Therapist (a blog about mental health issues surrounding work in Biglaw and what it's like to work with attorney patients run by former attorney and licensed clinical social worker Will Meyerhofer).

7. According to the Oregon Attorney Assistance Program (OAAP), attorneys in recovery have fewer disciplinary complaints and lower rates of malpractice (Sweeney 2002). The OAAP surveyed 55 attorneys five years before and five years after recovery; in the five years pre-recovery, there were 76 disciplinary complaints and 83 malpractice claims among the attorneys, while in the five years post-recovery there was a substantial decrease showing only 20 disciplinary complaints and 21 malpractice

claims (Sweeney 2002). The OAAP determined that effective treatment can help attorneys stay out of trouble.

8. For more information on LAPs please see the appendix for a listing with additional details of each state's LAP (see appendix online).

9. Depending on the state, this list may also include Licensed Professional Counselors (LPCs), Licensed Mental Health Counselors (LMHCs), Marriage and Family Therapists (MFTs), Licensed Professional Clinical Counselors (LPCCs), and Certified Alcohol Drug Counselor (CADCs). Check with your state to find out more.

10. Some attorneys in our sample of cases sought treatment within days of their disciplinary hearings and received mitigation. Of course, whether an attorney is afforded mitigation depends on the case but when time is of the essence it appears seeing a mental health practitioner in private practice may be the most convenient method to get help quickly.

11. This means that an impaired attorney who voluntarily (and properly) withdraws from a case and seeks mental health treatment does not need to notify the state bar; in essence, this attorney would be able to get help, maintain their privacy regarding treatment, and avoid discipline. On the other hand, an impaired attorney who fails to withdraw may end up being referred to the state bar for disciplinary action which could result in a referral for mental health services and could very well result in a public notice regarding the attorney's treatment.

Chapter 9

Future Recommendations

Though we have come a long way in the past decade in terms of understanding the depth of attorney mental health and substance use issues, there is still a long way to go. The ABA/Hazelden study (Krill et al. 2016) launched a movement in attorney mental health that we welcome and wish to build on. It is with this in mind that we discuss future recommendations in light of mental health and substance use in attorney disciplinary case data.

BEING AN EMPATHIC ATTORNEY

Our first recommendation, increasing empathy, is at the top of our list of changes we hope the legal profession takes up in the coming years. Empathy has been shown to be useful in a range of professions including social workers (Gerdes and Segal 2011), physicians (Decety 2020; Thangarasu, Renganthan, and Natarajan 2021), engineers (Hosking et al. 2015), and dairy farmers (Kielland et al. 2010). Indeed, more than likely, the benefits of being a more empathic individual may be universally felt across most professions and disciplines with lawyering as no exception.

This overarching recommendation to be more empathic is far easier said than done and has been called upon within the legal profession before (Barkai and Fine 1983; Henderson 1987; Massaro 1989). Despite recommendations throughout the years to increase empathy in the field, there has been a reluctance to embrace a more humanistic approach. Some legal scholars like Daicoff (2004, 28) astutely noted, ". . . individuals who are more people-oriented . . . are more likely to either drop out of law school. . . or be dissatisfied as attorneys." In other words, the students who graduate and go on to become attorneys may be less predisposed to having empathy. Dissatisfaction with the law may be more pronounced for individuals high on empathy too given that legal education focuses on the non-empathic thought process commonly referred to as "thinking like a lawyer."

What has been suggested then is learning how not to think like a lawyer. According to Syracuse University law professor Ian Gallacher (2010), empathy, a critical "professional tool" (36), should be taught as a "core lawyering skill" (1). Empathy, Gallacher (2010) said, can be strategized just as any other part of a legal case and has the benefit of helping the user be more in touch with themselves.[1] The notion that empathy should be a foundational element in training for a job that relies heavily on interpersonal skills makes sense; as a parallel, graduate school training in the mental health field emphasizes the role of empathy in several therapeutic approaches.[2] Creating a warmer environment in legal education could set the stage for students to become more empathic attorneys for their clients as well as when interacting with each other.

This brings us to disciplinary actions where attorneys are placed in a position where they must judge each other. As we mentioned in the case example perspectives, empathy felt conspicuously absent in our exploration of disciplinary records, and it is no wonder given the often adversarial and competitive culture of lawyering. We believe increasing empathy at the disciplinary court and state bar level is vital and would shift the therapeutic stance from a punitive tone to a more rehabilitative one. How we deal with mental health and substance use problems in attorneys could be transformed if hearing panel and disciplinary board members empathized with the attorneys who come before them.

Aside from empathy, three fundamental areas for future recommendations emerged as we reviewed our research and past literature on attorney mental health. These were:

REDESIGNING LAW SCHOOL

For changes within the profession to take root, we recommend several modifications at the law school level. One recommendation is to reassess law school admissions criteria to ensure candidates who are accepted possess relevant and desirable characteristics. Lawyering is based on fundamental "people skills" (Jolly-Ryan 2009, 118) such as empathy, collaboration, and an understanding of human suffering and as such, the legal profession would best be served to increase the number of graduates who have these characteristics. Adding more individuals with strong people skills in the profession could help transform the field from within and reach all the way to the disciplinary boards.

As gatekeepers of the profession, admissions committees should modify their admissions practices to be more in line with other graduate training, such as medical school or graduate school, where an applicant interview is conducted. Interviewing law school applicants, while time-consuming, would not only yield relevant information on the student's compatibility with the legal profession but also allow admissions committees to get a feel for what it would be like to be a client of that applicant. Feeling what it is like to sit with another human being is a useful tool mental health clinicians regularly employ and one which may not be used enough in the law. It would be beneficial to the profession as a whole if admissions committees spent more time investigating an applicant's intangibles: only so much information can be gleaned from GPA and LSAT scores.[3] After all, meeting in person is generally the best way to assess an individual's communication abilities and should be implemented in a profession where people skills are prioritized.

There are additional recommendations for law schools to consider once an applicant is admitted. After admission but before starting formal studies, Gallacher (2010) argues that law schools should implement an "informal and voluntary plan of study" such as a pre-law school course geared for incoming law students to help them shift into law school. Preparing students before beginning legal training could be beneficial as a way of inoculating them to the rigors of thinking like a lawyer. It could also serve as a demarcation between the end of undergraduate school and the beginning of law school which has been a potential trigger for mental health problems for some former law school students as we have discussed previously.

Law schools should also do more to address students' unrealistic and possibly damaging underlying beliefs about law career goals and what it takes to succeed in the law (Danmeyer and Nunez 1999). Law professors can help by normalizing struggles in law school and encouraging students to seek help if they notice problems. Law schools would be better served to promote a feeling of belonging among students through social activities which has been correlated with reduced levels of stress, anxiety, and depression (Skead and Rogers 2014). Self-care workshops should be offered alongside clinics to teach law students about well-being long before they feel the effects of burnout (Tyler 2016).

ALTERING THE STATE BAR

As discussed previously the ABA has been working to make changes that are consistent with CoLAP and the Task Force's (2017) recommendations[4] but more still needs to be done at the state bar level where attorneys with mental health and substance use issues are disciplined. To start with, in our view drug crimes are not and should not be considered crimes involving moral turpitude or acts of intentional dishonesty. We have observed in our cases that both the state bar courts and disciplinary boards view issues of misappropriation, concealment, fraud, and conversion as mutually exclusive from mental illness or substance use despite evidence to the contrary. It is as if licensing regulation bodies narrowly assume an act of dishonesty only has one meaning and therefore only one appropriate outcome (e.g., disbarment). Because of the severe penalties associated with these acts, many attorneys who suffer from serious mental illness or a severe substance use disorder have been disbarred from the profession. In comparison, the discipline of physicians offers another perspective on how we may want to improve our own regulatory system. As Heumann, Pinaire, and Lerman (2007) noted, physicians, even ones who are convicted of crimes, enjoy less severe penalties than attorneys and are afforded opportunities to return to practice should they wish.

Inferring a dishonest motive from behavior and using it to punish reminds us of cases where scienter, or an intent to commit a wrongdoing, has been inferred from a defendant's action and they are punished accordingly. We would discourage, however, using this same logic when it comes to attorneys who have mental health or substance use issues and are referred for discipline. We believe any attorney who submits evidence of their mental health or substance use issues should have their proof carefully examined before considering sanctions. Unless we wish to dismiss an individual's plea for help as unworthy of review, the complexities of their health and the high stakes involved necessitate a thorough understanding of the case factors involved.

Several other changes at the state bar level should be contemplated. Kratovil (2000) for one argues that before a disciplinary case proceeds we should determine whether the ADA applies to the attorney based on their evidence, and if so, implement a balancing test to consider multiple factors about the case. Analyzing applicability of the ADA in each attorney disciplinary case that asserts a qualifying diagnosis would provide for more consistent treatment of current standards. Once an attorney presents evidence of a diagnosis, eliminating the show of causation in mitigation factors for mental illness and substance use disorders would further be a step in the right direction as it creates too high a standard for ill individuals to meet (Rush 2011). As the California court criticized in *In the Matter of Lawrence* (2013), ". . . to require evidence that a disability or illness has 'permanently vanished' places too high a burden on an attorney. . . " (12). The court in *Lawrence* justly recognized the attorney's medical issues which involved neuralgia and a traumatic brain injury were unlikely to resolve completely. We believe this same understanding should be applied to significant mental health and substance use problems.

RECOMMENDATIONS FOR ATTORNEYS

First, we recommend that attorneys seek help *immediately* after identifying there is a problem and an accompanying impairment. Getting help, one of the first steps in recovery, is critical when it comes to healing[5] and potentially defending oneself in future disciplinary proceedings. In line with obtaining help, our sample of cases showed that agreeing to enter into a contract with a state bar association's LAP has been recognized as an asset in the eyes of Disciplinary Boards. Participating in treatment or monitoring through LAP does not guarantee a lesser sanction, but it does appear to possibly protect against receiving harsher punishment as it is commonly assigned some form of mitigation.

A vital piece to consider if an attorney is scheduled to attend a meeting with a hearing committee is to present live testifying witnesses. Given what we have learned from the pandemic, remote video testimony could work and possibly open up more opportunities for treating clinicians to testify. Asking witnesses to testify on the attorney's behalf as to any observations about the attorney's impairment has been shown to be highly beneficial for mitigation. In addition to expert witnesses, it would be helpful to present testimony of colleagues or coworkers who can speak as to how the attorney was functioning outside in their day-to-day lives at the office or outside of work. Observations from eyewitnesses can be invaluable when an impaired attorney wants to demonstrate the impact that their condition had on their work.

For attorneys working with clients that carry higher levels of trauma, more careful attention should be paid to signs of burnout and compassion fatigue. In addition to implementing CoLAP's (2019) well-being template and forming a committee or work group to discuss mental health issues, employers can help their staff by reducing caseloads for attorneys who have more traumatized clients, rotating or balancing out caseloads, or offering more support and counseling for at-risk staff members (Levin et al. 2012). Attorneys for their part should continue to establish healthy boundaries at their jobs when faced with challenging clients or opposing counsel where they defer to a judge or arbiter more often, adjourn a deposition or meeting that becomes too triggering, or file a motion to compel or protective orders sooner rather than later (Fisher and Adelman 2016).

A NEW MODEL FOR STATE BAR
DISCIPLINARY ACTIONS

As a final recommendation we would like to urge for an overhaul of the current framework of attorney discipline. While writing this book we had discussed how a therapeutic jurisprudence-type system could work with attorney regulation but have also come to understand other approaches could also be helpful. For example, some legal scholars have argued for a restorative justice approach to replace the current disciplinary system. Restorative justice, according to Hott and Waugh (2020), could offer a new foundation focused on healing attorneys through collaboration and righting wrongs. A new therapeutically-oriented approach, as opposed to the current system built largely on deterrence and veiled punitive mechanisms, should be implemented as a rehabilitative model committed to treating the profession and the individuals who work in it. With a new system, we hope that communication between law and mental health becomes more seamless and results in better, more empathic outcomes for society's advocates. There will need to be change at all levels, from law school to the courtroom. Only then can the profession truly heal the wounded attorney.

NOTES

1. For attorneys who are burned out or deal with the effects of compassion fatigue, a variation of empathy that has been recommended is developing a "detached concern" which allows for a healthy space between attorney and client (Small 2011).

2. Humanistic, existential, solution-focused brief therapy, relational therapy, and motivational interviewing are just some of the theoretical orientations that explicitly mention a focus on empathy in the therapy.

3. Many law school applicants have used the website lawschoolnumbers.com which compiles applicant submissions of GPA and LSAT scores to show what "numbers" have been accepted by a particular law school, emphasizing the idea that numbers are more important than anything else when it comes to admission decisions.

4. The ABA (2017) outlined several recommendations for stakeholders, judges, regulators, legal employers, law schools, bar associations, lawyers professional liability carriers, and lawyers assistance programs but there were no specific recommendations (unless you count 22.4 on Diversion Programs which were already in place before the report came out) for hearing committees or disciplinary boards who are responsible for recommending actions against attorneys.

5. In conjunction with seeking help, engaging in self-care should be a part of every individual's routine. Mental health recommendations for self-care include doing something different and away from work, socializing with a support network outside

of work, engaging in hobbies, and taking time off to nourish other parts of the brain as a way of revitalizing one's self (Norton et al. 2016). Mindfulness has also been shown to be therapeutic for law students (Scott 2018) and attorneys alike (Huang 2017).

References

Afana, Abdel-hamid, Odd Steffen Dalgad, Espen Bjertness, and Berthold Grunfeld. 2002. "The Ability of General Practitioners to Detect Mental Disorders Among Primary Care Patients in a Stressful Environment: Gaza Strip." *Journal of Public Health Medicine* 24, (4): 326–331.

Akhtar, Allana and Rebecca Aydin. 2019. "Some of the Jobs Most at Risk for Suicide and Depression Are the Most Important to Society. Here's a Rundown of Mental-Health Risks for Doctors, Childcare Workers, First Responders, and More." *Business Insider*, November 14, 2019. www.businessinsider.com/jobs-with-mental-health-risks-like-suicide-depression-2019-10.

Alfini, James J., and Joseph N. Van Vooren. 1995. "Is There a Solution to the Problem of Lawyer Stress? The Law School Perspective." *Journal of Law and Health* 10, no. 1: 61–67.

American Bar Association. 1992. "Standards for Imposing Lawyer Sanctions." Amended February 1992. www.americanbar.org/content/dam/aba/administrative/professional_responsibility/sanction_standards.pdf.

American Bar Association. 2018. "Report from the National Task Force on Lawyer Well-Being." Commission on Lawyer Assistance Programs, November 9, 2018. www.americanbar.org/groups/lawyer_assistance/task_force_report/.

American Bar Association. 2020a. "2018 Survey on Lawyer Discipline Systems (S.O.L.D.)." Standing Committee on Professional Regulation of the American Bar Association Center for Professional Responsibility, July 2020. www.americanbar.org/content/dam/aba/administrative/professional_responsibility/2018sold-results.pdf.

American Bar Association. 2020b. "ABA National Lawyer Population Survey: 10-Year Trend in Lawyer Population by State." www.americanbar.org/content/dam/aba/administrative/market_research/national-lawyer-population-demographics-2010-2020.pdf.

American Bar Association. 2020c. "ABA National Lawyer Population Survey: Lawyer Population by State." www.americanbar.org/resources_for_lawyers/profession_statistics.html.

157

American Bar Association. 2020d. "Mental Health Provisions in State Bar Exams." Commission on Disability Rights, current as of 2020. www.americanbar.org/content/dam/aba/administrative/commission-disability-rights/mh-provisions-state-bar-exams.pdf.

American Bar Association. 2020e. "Model Rules for Lawyer Disciplinary Enforcement." Last modified July 20, 2020. www.americanbar.org/groups/professional_responsibility/resources/lawyer_ethics_regulation/model_rules_for_lawyer_disciplinary_enforcement/.

American Bar Association. 2020f. "Model Rules of Professional Conduct." www.americanbar.org/groups/professional_responsibility/publications/model_rules_of_professional_conduct/model_rules_of_professional_conduct_table_of_contents/.

American Bar Association. 2020g. "Profile of the Legal Profession." www.americanbar.org/content/dam/aba/administrative/news/2020/07/potlp2020.pdf.

American Psychiatric Association. 2013. *Diagnostic and Statistical Manual of Mental Disorders - Fifth Edition*. Washington, D.C.: American Psychiatric Publishing.

Americans with Disabilities Act of 1990. 42 U.S.C. § 12101.

Anonymous. 2007. "Also Inside. . .: Quality of Life: Substance Abuse." *Louisiana Bar Journal* 55: 184.

Averitt, Hannah V. 2004. "A Mental Bar: Should Past Psychological Problems Affect Bar Admission?" *Law & Psychology Review* 28: 97.

Bahn, Josephine M. 2019. "New Mitigating Factor for Attorney Misconduct." American Bar Association. www.americanbar.org/groups/litigation/publications/litigation-news/top-stories/2019/new-mitigating-factor-attorney-misconduct/.

Banta, Carol J. 1995. "The Impact of the Americans with Disabilities Act on State Bar Examiners' Inquiries Into the Psychological History of Bar Applicants." *Michigan Law Review* 94, no. 1: 167–190.

Barkai, John L., and Virginia O. Fine. 1983. "Empathy Training for Lawyers and Law Students." *Southwestern University Law Review* 13: 505–529.

Barnhill, John W. 2018. "The Initial Interview." In *Co-Occurring Mental Illness and Substance Use Disorders: A Guide to Diagnosis and Treatment*, edited by Jonathan D. Avery and John W. Barnhill, 3–12. Arlington, Virginia: American Psychiatric Association Publishing.

Baron, Paula, and Lillian Corbin. 2019. "Lawyers, mental illness, admission and misconduct." *Legal Ethics* 22, no. 1–2: 28–48. doi: 10.1080/1460728x.2019.1692510.

Barrett, Sebrina A. 2017. "#Lawyervacay." *Journal of the Missouri Bar* 73 (4): 194.

Beck, Connie J. A., Bruce D. Sales, and G. Andrew H. Benjamin. 1995. "Lawyer Distress: Alcohol-Related Problems and Other Psychological Concerns Among a Sample of Practicing Lawyers." *Journal of Law and Health* 10, no. 1: 1–60.

Benjamin, G., and Andrew H. 1985. "Psychological Distress in Law Students and Lawyers." Paper presented at the 93rd Annual Convention of the American Psychological Association, Los Angeles, CA, August 23–27. Educational Resources Information Center copy.

Benjamin, G. Andrew H., Elain J. Darling, and Bruce Sales. 1990. "The Prevalence of Depression, Alcohol Abuse, and Cocaine Abuse Among United States

Lawyers." *International Journal of Law and Psychiatry* 13, no. 3: 233–246. doi: 10.1016/0160-2527(90)90019-y.

Berens, Michael, and John Schiffman. 2020. "Thousands of U.S. Judges Who Broke Laws or Oaths Remained on the Bench." Part 1: Objections Overruled. Reuters Investigates. www.reuters.com/investigates/special-report/usa-judges-misconduct/.

Berger, Brenda. 2000. Prisoners of Liberation: A Psychoanalytic Perspective on Disenchantment and Burnout among Career Women Lawyers." *JCLP/In Session: Psychotherapy in Practice* 56 (5): 665–673.

Bergin, Adele, and Kenneth, Pakenham. 2015. "Law student stress: Relationships Between Academic Demands, Social Isolation, Career Pressure, Study/Life Imbalance and Adjustment Outcomes in Law Students." *Psychiatry, Psychology & Law* 22 (3): 388–406. doi: 10.1080/13218719.2014.960026.

Blenkiron, Paul. 1999. Who is Suitable for Cognitive Behavioural Therapy? *Journal of the Royal Society of Medicine* 92: 222–229.

Bloom, Michael. A., and Carol Lynn Wallinger. 1988. "Lawyers and Alcoholism: Is it Time For a New Approach?" *Temple Law Review* 61: 1409–1413.

Bornstein, Brian H. 2009. "Physical v. Mental Pain: A Legal Double Standard?" *Monitor on Psychology* 40, no. 2: 18. www.apa.org/monitor/2009/02/jn.

Boughton, Melissa. 2020. "Uncharted Territory: Solo Attorneys, Small law Firms Struggle with Impacts of COVID-19." *NC Policy Watch*, April 30, 2020. www.ncpolicywatch.com/2020/04/30/uncharted-territory-solo-attorneys-small-law-firms-struggle-with-impacts-of-covid-19/.

Bowers, Stacey. L. 2010. "Library anxiety of law students: A study utilizing the Multidimensional Library Anxiety Scale." PhD diss., University of Denver.

Bray, Bethany. 2021. "The Future of Telehealth: Looking Ahead." *Counseling Today*, April 22, 2021. ct.counseling.org/2021/04/the-future-of-telehealth-looking-ahead/.

Brobst, Jennifer. 2014. "The Impact of Secondary Traumatic Stress Among Family Attorneys Working with Trauma-Exposed Clients: Implications for Practice and Professional Responsibility." *Journal of Health & Biomedical Law* 10: 1–53.

Brooke, Deborah. 1997. "Impairment in the Medical and Legal Professions." *Journal of Psychosomatic Research* 43, no. 1: 27–34.

Burge, Kristen L. 2017. "Automatic Disbarment: A Sobering Reality for Convicted Attorneys." *American Bar Association*, February 17, 2017. https://www.americanbar.org/groups/litigation/publications/litigation-news/top-stories/2017/automatic-disbarment-sobering-reality-convicted-attorneys/.

Butler County v. Blauvelt, 156 N.E.3d 891 (2020).

Centers for Disease Control and Prevention. 2020. Disability Impacts All of Us. www.cdc.gov/ncbddd/disabilityandhealth/documents/disabilities_impacts_all_of_us.pdf.

Chamberlain, Jared, and Monica K. Miller. 2009. "Evidence of Secondary Traumatic Stress, Safety Concerns, and Burnout Among a Homogenous Group of Judges in a Single Jurisdiction." *The Journal of the American Academy of Psychiatry and the Law* 37, no. 2: 214–224.

Chartier, Doug. 2019. "The Therapist Down the Hall: A Look into Hogan Lovells' On-Site Counseling Program." Law Week Colorado 17, no. 5: 12–13.

Chen, Vivia. 2020. "For Women Lawyers, Marriage Sucks." *Law.com*, March 10, 2020. www.law.com/americanlawyer/2020/03/10/for-women-lawyers-marriage-sucks/.

Childers, Hon. Robert L. "Butch." 2009. "Chair's Column Women and Recovery" Highlights Newsletter.

Chiles, John A., G. Andrew H. Benjamin, and Timothy S. Cahn. 1990. "Who Smokes? Why?: Psychiatric Aspects of Continued Cigarette Usage Among Lawyers in Washington State." *Comprehensive Psychiatry* 31, no. 2: 176–184. doi: 10.1016/0010-440x(90)90022-k.

Chinaris, Timothy P. 2005. "Even Judges Don't Know Everything: A Call for a Presumption of Admissibility for Expert Witness Testimony in Lawyer Disciplinary Proceedings. *St. Mary's Law Journal* 36, no. 4: 825–878.

Cho, Jenna. 2017. "Why Lawyers Fear Seeing Therapists, and Why We Should Do It Anyway." *Above the Law*, May 22, 2017. abovethelaw.com/2017/05/why-lawyers-fear-seeing-therapists-and-why-we-should-do-it-anyway/.

Cincinnati Bar Association v. Fernandez, 119 N.E.3d 377 (2018).

Clarke, Brian. 2014. "How I Almost Became Another Lawyer Who Killed Himself." North Carolina Lawyer Assistance Program. www.nclap.org/almost-became-another-lawyer-killed/.

Clow, Kristen. 2020. "Mental Health and the Character and Fitness Examination: The Tide is Shifting." *North Dakota Law Review* 95, no. 2: 327–344.

Columbus Bar Association v. Elsass, 713 N.E.2d 421 (1999).

Commission on Lawyer Assistance Programs and Working Group to Advance Well-Being in the Legal Profession. 2019. "Well-Being Template for Legal Employers." American Bar Association. www.americanbar.org/content/dam/aba/administrative/lawyer_assistance/well-being-template-for-legal-employers-final-3-19.pdf.

Commission on Lawyer Assistance Programs. 2020a. "Case Law Reviews." Last Updated October 5, 2020. www.americanbar.org/groups/lawyer_assistance/resources/case_law_reviews/.

Commission on Lawyer Assistance Programs. 2020b. "Directory of Lawyer Assistance Programs." American Bar Association. www.americanbar.org/groups/lawyer_assistance/resources/lap_programs_by_state/.

Commission on Lawyer Assistance Programs. 2020c. "Drug Use Disorders." American Bar Association, January 13, 2021. www.americanbar.org/groups/lawyer_assistance/resources/drug_abuse_dependence/.

Confino, Jordana Alter. 2019. "Where Are We on the Path to Law Student Law-Being?: Report on the ABA CoLAP Law Student Assistance Committee Law School Wellness Survey." *Journal of Legal Education* 68, no. 3: 650–715.

Congressional Research Service. 2021. "Unemployment Rates During the COVID-19 Pandemic." Report No. R46554, updated May 20, 2021. fas.org/sgp/crs/misc/R46 554.pdf.

Curtis, Debra Moss, and Billie Jo Kaufman. 2004. "A Public View of Attorney Discipline in Florida: Statistics, Commentary, and Analysis of Disciplinary Actions Against Licensed Attorneys in the State of Florida from 1988–2002." *Nova Law Review* 28: 669–719.

Daicoff, Susan Swaim. 2004. *Lawyer Know Thyself: A Psychological Analysis of Personality Strengths and Weaknesses*. Washington, D.C: American Psychological Association.

Danmeyer, Matthew M., and Narina Nunez. 1999. "Anxiety and Depression Among Law Students: Current Knowledge and Future Directions." *Law and Human Behavior* 23, no. 1: 55–73.

The Dave Nee Foundation. www.daveneefoundation.org.

Davis-Laack, Paula. 2020. "Burned Out Bosses." Stress and Resilience Institute. stressandresilience.com/burned-out-bosses/.

Decety, Jean. 2020. "Empathy in Medicine: What It Is, and How Much We Really Need It." *The American Journal of Medicine* 133, no. 5: 561–566. doi: 10.1016/j.amjmed.2019.12.012.

Disciplinary Board v. Summers, 817 N.W.2d 363 (2012).

Disciplinary Counsel v. Adelstein, 159 N.E.3d 1126 (2020).

Disciplinary Counsel v. Karp, 124 N.E.3d 819 (2018).

Disciplinary Proceeding against Petersen, 846 P.2d 1330 (1993).

Doe v. Kentucky. 2020. Civil Action No. 3:19-CV-236-JRW (filed 08/28/20).

Dutton, Kevin. 2013. *The Wisdom of Psychopaths: What Saints, Spies, and Serial Killers Can Teach Us About Success*. New York: Scientific American.

Eaton, William, W., James C. Anthony, Wallace Mandel, and Roberta Garrison. 1990. "Occupations and the Prevalence of Major Depressive Disorder." *Journal of Occupational Medicine* 32, no. 11: 1079–1087.

Eckholm, Erik. 2008. "Citing Workload, Public Defenders Reject New Cases." *The New York Times*, November 8, 2008. www.nytimes.com/2008/11/09/us/09defender.html.

Edwards, Jean C. 2018. "Incidence of Bar Discipline in Millennial Attorneys." Master thesis, Harvard University.

Fabian, John D., and Brian Reinthaler. 2001. "An Examination of the Uniformity (or Lack Thereof) of Attorney Sanctions." *Georgetown Journal Legal Ethics* 14: 1059–1080.

Felder, Corie Rosen. 2014. "The Accidental Optimist." *Virginia Journal of Social Policy & the Law* 21 (1): 63–99.

Fines, Barbara Glesner, and Cathy Madsen. 2007. Caring Too Little, Caring Too Much: Competence and the Family Law Attorney. Symposium: Ethics of Family Law Representation. *University of Missouri-Kansas City Law Review* 75: 965–998.

Fisher, Paul, and Adelman, Juli. 2016. "Managing Dismissive and Bully Opposing Attorneys." *Probate & Property* 30, no. 4 (Jul/Aug).

Flanagan, Rebecca. 2008. "Lucifer Goes to Law School: Towards Explaining and Minimizing Law Student Peer-to-Peer Harassment and Intimidation." *Washburn Law Journal* 47: 453.

Flores, David M., Monica K. Miller, Jared Chamberlain, James T. Richardson, and Brian H. Bornstein. 2009. "Judges' Perspective on Stress and Safety in the Courtroom: An Exploratory Study." *Court Review* 45: 76–88.

Flores, Philip J. 2004. *Addiction as an Attachment Disorder*. Jason Aronson: Lanham, M.D.

Florida v. Little. (2018). Supreme Court of Florida. Case No. SC18–479, filed July 20, 2018.

The Florida Bar. 2021. "Lawyer Discipline Statistics." www.floridabar.org/public/acap/lawyer-discipline-statistics/.

Flynn, Andrea M., Yan Li, and Bernadette Sánchez. 2019. "The Mental Health Status of Law Students: Implications for College Counselors." *Journal of College Counseling* 22, no. 1: 2–12. doi: 10.1002/jocc.12110.

Fortney, Susan Saab. 2000. "Soul for Sale: An Empirical Study of Associate Satisfaction, Law Firm Culture, and the Effects of Billable Hour Requirements." *University of Missouri-Kansas City Law Review* 69: 239–309.

Freudenberger, Herbert, and Geraldine Richelson. 1980. *Burn Out: The High Cost of Achievement*. New York: Bantam Books.

Gallacher, Ian. 2010. Thinking Like Non-Lawyers: Why Empathy is a Core Lawyering Skill and Why Legal Education Should Change to Reflect Its Importance. *Journal of the Association of Legal Writing Directors*, 1–49. surface.syr.edu/cgi/viewcontent.cgi?article=1005&context=lawpub.

Gates, C. 2008. Division's first annual National Mental Health Day a success. *Student Lawyer* 37 no. 2: 34.

Gentry, J. Eric. 2002. "Compassion Fatigue: A Crucible of Transformation." *Journal of Trauma Practice* 1, no. 3/4: 37–61. doi: 10.1300/j189v01n03_03.

Gerdes, Karen E., and Elizabeth Segal. 2011. "Importance of Empathy for Social Work Practice: Integrating New Science." *Social Work* 56, No. 2 (April): 141–148. dx.doi.org/10.1093/sw/56.2.141.

Gillander, Ellen. 2018. "Bearing Witness to Crime: An Examination of Secondary Traumatic Stress and Vicarious Trauma among Attorneys." PsyD diss., William James College.

Gillers, Stephen. 2014. "Lowering the Bar: How Lawyer Discipline in New York Fails to Protect the Public." *N.Y.U. Journal of Legislation & Public Policy* 17: 485–541.

Gillespie, Anusha. 2021. "The Horrible Conflict Between Biology and Women Attorneys." American Bar Association. www.americanbar.org/careercenter/blog/the-horrible-conflict-between-biology-and-women-attorneys/.

Goldberg, Stephanie B. 1990. "Drawing the Line - When Is an Ex-Coke Addict Fit to Practice Law?" *ABA Journal* 76, no. 2: 49–53.

Goldstein, Mark S. 2019. "'Scared. Ashamed. Crippled.': How One Lawyer Overcame Living with Depression in Big Law." *Law.com*, February 12, 2019. www.law.com/americanlawyer/2019/02/12/scared-ashamed-crippled-how-one-lawyer-overcame-living-with-depression-in-big-law/.

Gomme, Ian M., and Mary P. Hall. 1995. "Prosecutors at Work: Role Overload and Strain." *Journal of Criminal Justice* 23, no. 2: 191–200. doi: 10.1016/0047-2352(95)00006-C.

Goodliffe, Jonathan. 1994. "Alcohol and Depression in English and American Lawyer Disciplinary Proceedings." *Addiction* 89, no. 10: 1237–1244. doi: 10.1111/j.1360-0443.1994.tb03302.x.

Goswamy, Ritu. 2019. *The New Billable Hour*. New York: Morgan James Publishing.

Gutierrez, Fernando. J. 1985. "Counseling Law Students." *Journal of Counseling & Development* 64, no. 2: 130–133. doi: 10.1002/j.1556-6676.1985.tb01051.x.

Hardegree, Lee. 1979. "Mental or Physical Incapacity as a Bar to the Practice of Law." *The Journal of the Legal Profession*, 219–226.

Hazilla, Kyra M. 2016. "Vicarious Trauma Primer for the Juvenile Court Practitioner. *Juvenile Law Reader* 13, no. 3. youthrightsjustice.org/wp-content/uploads/reader-archive/Juvenile_Law_Reader_13–3.pdf.

Heil, Patricia Sue. 1993. "Tending the Bar in Texas: Alcoholism as a Mitigating Factor in Attorney Discipline." *St. Mary's Law Journal* 24: 1263–1297.

Henderson, Lynne N. 1987. "Legality and Empathy." *Michigan Law Review* 85: 1574–1653.

Herr, Stanley S. 1997. "Questioning the Questionnaires: Bar Admissions and Candidates with Disabilities." *Villanova Law Review* 42: 635–722.

Heumann, Milton, Brian Pinaire, and Jennifer Lerman. 2007. "Prescribing Justice: The law and Politics of Discipline for Physician Felony Offenders." *Boston University Public Interest Law Journal* 17, no. 1: 1–38.

Hosking, Ian, Katie Cornish, Mike Bradley, and P. John Clarkson. 2015. "Empathic Engineering: Helping Deliver Dignity through Design." *Journal of Medical Engineering & Technology* 39, no. 7: 388–394. doi: 10.3109/03091902.2015.1088090.

Hott, Rachel N., and Brenda Waugh. 2020. "Discipline Does Not Make an Ill Lawyer Well," . . . But Can It?: Creating Effective, Consumer Friendly and Human Lawyer Discipline Systems by Adopting Principles, Values and Processes Rooted in Restorative Justice. *Richmond Public Interest Law Review* 23: 243–266.

Huang, Peter H. 2017. "Can Practicing Mindfulness Improve Lawyer Decision-Making, Ethics, and Leadership?" *Houston Law Review* 55, no. 1: 63–154.

Hudson, David L. 2016. "Honesty is the Best Policy for Character-and-Fitness Screenings. *ABA Journal*, June 1, 2016. www.abajournal.com/magazine/article/honesty_is_the_best_policy_for_character_and_fitness_screenings.

———. 2020. "Disbarred Attorneys Trying to Get Their Licenses Back Face an Uphill Battle." *ABA Journal*. abajournal.com/magazine/article/disbarred-attorneys-trying-to-get-their-licenses-back-face-an-uphill-battle.

Human Rights. 1992. "Study Tracks State and Local Bar Programs." 19, no. 1 (Winter).

In re Abdalla, 2017-B-0453 (La. 10/18/17); 236 So. 3d 1223.

In re Griffiths, 413 U.S. 717 (1973).

In re Jordan, 421 S.C. 594 (2017).

In re Kupka, 458 P.3d 242 (2020).

In re Miller, 223 A.3d 976 (2020).

In re Perricone, 263 So. 3d 309 (2018).

In re Perricone, Louisiana Attorney Disciplinary Board. No. 17-DB-016. Filed July 17, 2018.

In re Salo, 48 A.3d 174 (2012).

In re Silva, 29 A.3d 924 (2011).

In re Steinbach, Iowa Supreme Court Order of Public Reprimand. No. 20–1356. Dated September 11, 2020.

In re Webb, 418 P.3d 2 (2018).

In re Wickersham, 310 P.3d 1237 (2013).

Institute for Well-Being in Law. 2021 lawyerwellbeing.net.

In the Matter of Amponsah, State Bar Court of California. Case Nos. 17-N-06871 and 17-O-06931 filed April 22, 2019.

In the Matter of Broderick, Indiana Supreme Court Case No. 19S-DI-476, filed September 10, 2020.

In the Matter of Guillory, Case Nos. 12-C-11576; 12-C-11759; 12-C-12032; 12-C-12883 (2015)

In the Matter of Lawrence. 2013. State Bar of California Review Department. Case Nos. 07-O-12696, 07-O-13600, 10-O-10811, filed March 12, 2013.

In the Matter of Lingwood. 2019. State Bar Court of California Review Department. Case No. 16-O-17302, filed August 27, 2019.

In the Matter of Peters, State Bar Court of California. Case No. 13-C-16396 filed January 29, 2018.

In the Matter of Piatt, Indiana Supreme Court Case No. 20S-DI-6, filed October 16, 2020.

In the Matter of Romano. 2015. State Bar Court of California Review Department. Case No. 12-J-15277, filed April 30, 2015.

Iowa v. Bergmann, 938 N.W.2d 16 (2020).

Iowa v. Cannon, 821 N.W.2d 873 (2012).

Iowa v. Kennedy, 837 N.W.2d 659 (2013).

Iowa v. Marks, 831 N.W.2d 194 (2013).

Johnson, Ruth Lee. 2014. "Are Lawyers All Raging Psychopaths?" *Psychology Today*, August 19, 2014. www.psychologytoday.com/us/blog/so-sue-me/201408/are-lawyers-all-raging-psychopaths.

Johnston, Erin. 2018. "How Do I Do It? Not All at Once, And Not All Alone." *ABA Journal*, November 2018. www.kirkland.com/publications/article/2018/11/how-do-i-do-it_not-all-at-once_and-not-all-alone.

Johnstone, Quintin. 2004. "Connecticut Unauthorized Practice Laws and Some Options for Their Reform." *Connecticut Law Review* 36: 303–351.

Jolly-Ryan, Jennifer. 2009. "Promoting Mental Health in Law School: What Law Schools Can Do for Law Students to Help Them Become Happy, Mentally Healthy Lawyers." *University of Louisville Law Review* 48, no. 1: 95–137.

Jones, James T. R. 2015. "High Functioning": Successful Professionals with Severe Mental Illness." *Duke Forum for Law & Social Change* 7, no. 1: 1–35.

Karabin, Sherry. 2015. "Shedding the Stigma of Mental Illness." *Student Lawyer* 43, no. 8 (April/May). abaforlawstudents.com/tag/april-may-2015/.

Kelk, Norm, Georgina Luscombe, Sharon Medlow, and Ian Hickie. 2009. "Courting the Blues: Attitudes towards depression in Australian law students and lawyers." University of Sydney Brain & Mind Research Institute.

Kielland, C., E. Skjerve, O. Østerås, and A. J. Zanella. 2010. "Dairy Farmer Attitudes and Empathy Toward Animals Are Associated with Animal Welfare Indicators." *Journal of Dairy Science* 93, no. 7: 2998–3006. doi: 10.3168/jds.2009-2899.

Kim, Jasper. 2011. *24 Hours with 24 Lawyers: Profiles of Traditional and Non-Traditional Careers*. USA: Thomson Reuters/Aspatore.

Kissam, Philip C. 1989. "Law School Examinations." *Vanderbilt Law Review* 42: 433–504.

Klingen, Len. 2002. "The Mentally Ill Attorney." *Nova Law Review* 27: 157–189.

Krakowski, Dr. Adam J. 1984. "Stress and the Practice of Medicine: Ill. Physicians Compared with Lawyers." *Psychotherapy and Psychosomatics* 42, no. 1–4:143–151.

Kratovil, Christopher D. 2000. "Separating Disability from Discipline: The ADA and Bar Discipline." *Texas Law Review* 78: 993–1013.

Krill, Patrick R., Ryan Johnson, and Linda Albert. 2016. "The Prevalence of Substance Use and Other Mental Health Concerns Among American Attorneys." *American Society of Addiction Medicine* 10, no. 1; 46–52. doi: 10.1097/ADM.0000000000000182.

Krill, Patrick. 2018. "What Do the Statistics About Lawyer Alcohol Use and Mental Health Problems *Really Mean?*" *The Florida Bar Journal* 92, no. 1: 10–12.

Krom, Cynthia L. 2019. "Disciplinary Actions by State Professional Licensing Boards: Are They Fair?" *Journal of Business Ethics* 158, no. 2: 567–583. doi: 10.1007/s10551-017-3738-5.

Law.com. 2021. *Mind Over Matters: An Examination of Mental Health in the Legal Profession*. Special Report. www.law.com/special-reports/minds-over-matters-an-examination-of-mental-health-in-the-legal-profession/.

Lawyer Disciplinary Board v. Sidiropolis, 241 W. Va. 777 (2019).

Leignel, S., J.-P. Schuster, N. Hoertel, X. Poulain, and F. Limosin. 2014. "Mental health and Substance Use Among Self-Employed Lawyers and Pharmacists." *Occupational Medicine* 64, no. 3: 166–171. doi: 10.1093/occmed/kqt173.

Levin, Andrew, Avi Besser, Linda Albert, Deborah Smith, and Yuval Neria. 2012. The Effect of Attorneys' Work with Trauma-Exposed Clients on PTSD Symptoms, Depression, and Functional Impairment: A Cross-Lagged Longitudinal Study." *Law and Human Behavior* 36, no. 6: 538–547. doi: 10.1037/h0093993.

Levin, Andrew P., Linda Albert, Avi Besser, Deobrah Smith, Alex Zelenski, Stacey Rosenkranz, and Yuval Neria. 2011. "Secondary Traumatic Stress in Attorneys and Their Administrative Support Staff Working with Trauma-Exposed Clients." *Journal of Nervous and Mental Disease* 199, no. 12: 946–955. doi: 10.1097/NMD.0b013e3182392c26.

Levin, Leslie C. 1998. "The Emperor's Clothes and Other Tales About the Standards for Imposing Lawyer Discipline Sanctions." *American University Law Review* 48, no. 1: 1–83. digitalcommons.wcl.american.edu/aulr/vol48/iss1/1.

———. "The Case for Less Secrecy in Lawyer Discipline." *Georgetown Journal of Legal Ethics* 20, no. 1: 1–50.

———. "The Folly of Expecting Evil: Reconsidering the Bar's Character and Fitness Requirement." *Brigham Young University Law Review* 2014, no. 4: 775–818.

Levin, Leslie C., Christine Zozula, and Peter Siegelman. 2015. "The Questionable Character of the Bar's Character and Fitness Inquiry." *Law & Social Inquiry* 40, no. 1: 51–85.

LexisNexis. 2018. "Write a Publishable Comment for Your Law Review or Journal." LexisNexis.com. www.lexisnexis.com/supp/lawschool/resources/write-a-publishable-comment.pdf.

Li, Zhenyu, Jingwu Ge, Meiling Yang, Jianping Feng, Mei Qiao, Riyue Jiang, Jiangjiang Bi, Gaofeng Zhan, Xiaolin Xu, Long Wang, Qin Zhou, Chenliang Zhou, Yinbing Pan, Shijian Liu, Haiwei Zhang, Jianjun Yang, Bin Zhu, Yimin Hu, Kenji Hashimoto, Yan Jia, Haofei Wang, Rong Wang, Cunming Liu, and Chun Yang. 2020. "Vicarious Traumatization in the General Public, Members, and Non-Members of Medical Teams Aiding in COVID-19 Control." *Brain, Behavior, and Immunity* 88: 916–919. doi: 10.1016/j.bbi.2020.03.007.

Luty, David. 2004. "In the Matter of Mitigation: The Necessity of a Less Discretionary Standard for Sanctioning Lawyers Found Guilty of Intentionally Misappropriating Client Property." *Hofstra Law Review* 32, no. 3: 999–1037.

Ly, Dan P., Seth A. Seabury, and Anupam B. Jena. 2015. "Divorce Among Physicians and Other Healthcare Professionals in the United States: Analysis of Census Survey Data." *British Medical Journal* 350, no. 7997: 706. doi: 10.1136/bmj.h706.

Mangan, Kate. 2015. "How to Recognize and Prevent Lawyer Burnout." *Lawyerist*, August 1, 2019. lawyerist.com/blog/recognize-prevent-lawyer-burnout/.

Markham, Lauren. 2020. "No End in Sight: What Happens When Immigrant-Rights Advocates Reach a Breaking Point?" *The Virginia Quarterly Review*, March 2, 2020. www.vqronline.org/reporting-articles/2020/03/no-end-sight?fbclid=IwAR1 TTnZfRjovuwpDsjCE833SqXHxqNi7w-54V1afyQa2BdWhdECYVfsB7Mw.

Maryland v. Miller, 223 A.3d 976 (2020).

Maslach, Christina. 1976. "Burnout." *Human Behavior* 5: 16–22.

Massaro, Toni M. 1989. "Legal Storytelling: Empathy, Legal Storytelling, and the Rule of Law: New Words, Old Wounds? *Michigan Law Review* 87: 2099–2127.

Matter of Bolduc, 990 N.Y.S.2d 93 (2014).

Matter of Cohen, 2019 NY Slip Op 01381. New York, 1st Department, Appellate Division. Decided February 26, 2019.

Matter of Goldstein, 995 N.Y.S.2d 111 (2014).

Matter of Hanrahan, 923 N.Y.S.2d 567 (2011).

Matter of Norton, 81 N.Y.S.3d 216 (2018).

Matter of Salo, 906 N.Y.S.2d 16 (2010).

Matter of Smith, 2019 NY Slip Op 03904. New York, 1st Department, Appellate Division. Decided May 16, 2019.

McCann, I. Lisa, and Laurie A. Pearlman. 1990. "Vicarious Traumatization: A Framework for Understanding the Psychological Effects of Working with Victims." *Journal of Traumatic Stress* 3, no. 1: 131–149. doi: 10.1007/BF00975140.

Miano, Steven T. 2015. "Views from the Chair: Networking that is Worth Your Time." *Trends* 46, no. 3: 24–25.

Milowec III, Joseph. 2018. "Quinn Emanuel Partner Suffers from Depression and He Wants Everyone to Know." *Law.com*, March 28, 2018. www. law.com/newyorklawjournal/2018/03/28/quinn-emanuel-partner-suffers-from-depression-and-he-wants-everyone-to-know/?slret urn=20210326005305.

Miranda, John. 2018. "Legally bombed: Young, Millennial Lawyers, Same Old Alcoholism." *ABA Journal*, October 9, 2018. www.abajournal.com/voice/article/legally_bombed_young_millennial_lawyers_same_old_alcoholism.

Mogill, Kenneth M. 2014. "Trial Practice: Trying an Attorney Discipline Case." *Michigan Bar Journal* 93: 44–45.

National Alliance on Mental Illness. 2021. "Mental Health by the Numbers." Updated March 2021. www.nami.org/mhstats.

National Association for Law Placement. 2016. "Update on Associate Hours Worked." *NALP Bulletin*. www.nalp.org/0516research.

National Association for Law Placement. 2018a. "Findings from the NALP/PSJD 2018 Public Service Attorney Salary Survey." *NALP Bulletin*, June 2018. https://www.nalp.org/0618research.

National Association for Law Placement. 2018b. "Salary Distribution Curves." www.nalp.org/salarydistrib.

National Association for Law Placement. 2019. "Report on Diversity in U.S. Law Firms."

www.nalp.org/uploads/2019_DiversityReport.pdf.

National Conference of Bar Examiners. 2021. "Comprehensive Guide to Bar Admission Requirements." reports.ncbex.org/comp-guide/code-of-recommended-standards/.

National Institute of Mental Health (NIH). https://www.nimh.nih.gov/index.shtml.

National Institute on Drug Abuse. 2010. "Comorbidity: Addiction and Other Mental Illnesses." National Institutes of Health Research Report Series, revised 2010. NIH publication number 10–5771. www.drugabuse.gov/sites/default/files/rrcomorbidity.pdf.

National Institute on Drug Abuse. 2020. "Treatment and recovery." Drugs, Brains, and Behavior: The Science of Addiction, NIH Publication No. 20-DA-5605, revised June 2020. www.drugabuse.gov/sites/default/files/soa.pdf.

National Public Radio Staff. 2015. "'Shots on the Bridge' Unpacks a Tangled Story of Deceit and Tragedy." *National Public Radio*, August 18, 2015. www.npr.org/2015/08/18/432570962/shots-on-the-bridge-unpacks-a-tangled-story-of-deceit-and-tragedy.

Neal, Hayley Easton. 2011. "Current Development 2010–2011: Evaluating the New York State Bar Association Lawyer Assistance Committee Model Policy." *Georgetown Journal of Legal Ethics* 24: 733–746.

Nebraska v. Person, 919 N.W.2d 856 (2018).

New York State Bar Committee on Professional Discipline. 2015. "Report and Recommendations Concerning Discovery in Disciplinary Proceedings." Issued June 26, 2015. nysba.org/app/uploads/2020/02/Final-Discovery-Report-approved-7-24-2015.pdf

Norton, Lee, Jennifer Johnson, and George Woods. 2016. "Burnout and Compassion Fatigue: What Lawyers Need to Know. *University of Missouri-Kansas City Law Review* 84, no. 4: 987–1002.

O'Connell, Diane. 2019. "A Big Firm Shouldn't Be Your Only Career Plan." New York State Bar Association, August 1, 2019. nysba.org/a-big-firm-shouldnt-be-your-only-career-plan/.

Oklahoma Bar Association v. Soderstrom, 321 P.3d 159 (2013).

Organ, Jerome, M., David B. Jaffe, and Katherine M. Bender. 2016. "Suffering in Silence: The Survey of Law Student Well-Being and the Reluctance of Law Students to Seek Help for Substance Use and Mental Health Concerns." *Journal of Legal Education* 66, no. 1: 116–156.

Pearson. 2021. "Minnesota Multiphasic Personality Inventory-2 (MMPI-2)." www.pearsonassessments.com/store/usassessments/en/Store/Professional-Assessments/Personality-%26-Biopsychosocial/Minnesota-Multiphasic-Personality-Inventory-2/p/100000461.html?tab=product-details.

The People's Therapist. thepeoplestherapist.com.

People v. Ward, 470 P.3d 1053 (2017).

Persky, Anna Stolley. 2014. "State Bars May Probe Applicants' Behavior, But Not Mental Health Status, says DOJ." *ABA Journal*, June 1, 2014. www.abajournal.com/magazine/article/state_bars_may_probe_applicants_behavior_but_not_mental_health_status.

Piquero, Nicole Leeper, Michele Bisaccia Meitl, Eve M. Brank, Jennifer L. Woolard, and Lonn Lanza-Kaduce. 2016. "Exploring Lawyer Misconduct: An Examination of the Self-Regulation Process." *Deviant Behavior* 37, no. 5: 573–584.

Pregenzer, Lynne. 1993. "Substance Abuse within the Legal Profession: A Symptom of a Greater Malaise." *Notre Dame Journal of Law, Ethics & Public Policy* 7, no. 1: 305–329. scholarship.law.nd.edu/ndjlepp/.

Rabkow, Nadja, Lilith Pukas, Alexandra Sapalidis, Emilia Ehring, Lea Keuch, Carolin Rehnisch, Oskar Feußner, Isabell Klima, and Stefan Watzke. 2020. "Facing the Truth—A Report on the Mental Health Situation of German Law Students." *International Journal of Law & Psychiatry* 71. doi: 10.1016/j.ijlp.2020.101599.

Reed, Krystia, Brian H. Bornstein, Andrew B. Jeon, and Lindsey E. Wylie. 2016. "Problem Signs in Law School: Fostering Attorney Well-Being Early in Professional Training." *International Journal of Law and Psychiatry* 47: 148–156.

Reifman, Alan, Daniel N. McLntosh, and Phoebe C. Ellsworth. 2001. "Depression and Affect Among Law Students During Law School. *Journal of Emotional Abuse* 2, no. 1: 93–106. doi: 10.1300/J135v02n01_07.

Resnick, Alexis, Karen A. Myatt, and Priscilla V. Marotta. 2011. "Surviving Bench Stress." *Family Court Review* 49, no. 3: 610–617. doi: 10.1111/j.1744-1617.2011.01396.x.

Rhode, Deborah L. 1985. "Moral Character as a Professional Credential." *The Yale Law Journal* 94, no. 3: 491–603. digitalcommons.law.yale.edu/cgi/viewcontent.cgi?article=6904&context=ylj.

Robinson, James Gray. 2020. "How Lawyers Can Manage Stress and Cortisol Levels During the COVID-19 Crisis." *ABA Journal*, April 22, 2020. www.abajournal.com/voice/article/why-lawyers-need-to-know-about-cortisol.

Robinson-Keilig, Rachael A. 2014. "Secondary Traumatic Stress and Disruptions to Interpersonal Functioning Among Mental Health Therapists." *Journal of Interpersonal Violence* 29, no. 8: 1477–1496. doi: 10.1177/0886260513507135.

Rodriguez, Natalie. 2018. "The Least Stressed Attorneys in a Stressed-Out Profession." *Law360 In-Depth*, July 23, 2018. www.law360.com/articles/1065415/the-least-stressed-attorneys-in-a-stressed-out-profession.

Rosen, Corie. 2011. "The Method and the Message." *Nevada Law Journal* 12, no. 1: 160–186. scholars.law.unlv.edu/nlj/vol12/iss1/7.

Rovzar, Alexander O. 2015. "Putting the Plug in the Jug: The Malady of Alcoholism and Substance Addiction in the Legal Profession and a Proposal for Reform." *University of Massachusetts Law Review* 10, no. 2: 426–463.

Rowe, Jr., Crayton E. 2009. "Psychophobia" is a Major Current Issue Affecting Psychoanalytic Training and Practice." *Clinical Social Work Journal* 37: 79–80. doi: 10.1007/s10615-008-0186-9.

Rubin, Karen. 2015. "Sex Addiction" Not a Mitigating Factor in Discipline: Ohio Court." *The Law for Lawyers Today*, July 16, 2015. www.thelawforlawyerstoday. com/2015/07/sex-addiction-not-a-mitigating-factor-in-discipline-ohio-court/.

Rubin, Karen. 2018. "Lawyer's 'Compassion Fatigue' Entitled to Little Weight; WA Court Disbars Him for Converting Client Funds, Other Misconduct." *The Law for Lawyers Today*, July 26, 2018. www.thelawforlawyerstoday.com/2018/07/lawyers-compassion-fatigue-entitled-to-little-weight-wa-court-disbars-him-for-converting-client-funds-other-misconduct/.

Rush, Judith. M. 2011. "Disbarment of Impaired Lawyers: Making the Sanction Fit the Crime. *William Mitchell Law Review* 37, no. 2: 916–949.

Skoler, Daniel L., and Roger M. Klein. 1979. "Mental Disability and Lawyer Discipline." *The John Marshall Journal of Practice and Procedure* 12, no. 2: 227–252.

South Carolina Judicial Department. 2021. "FY 2018–2019." Commission on Lawyer Conduct Annual Reports. www.sccourts.org/discCounsel/CLC2019.pdf.

Substance Abuse and Mental Health Services Administration. 2014. "More Than One Third of Adults with Major Depressive Episode Did Not Talk to a Professional." *The NSDUH Report*, February 20, 2014.

Substance Abuse and Mental Health Services Administration. 2018. "Key Substance Use and Mental Health Indicators in the United States: Results from the 2018 National Survey on Drug Use and Health." U.S. Department of Health and Human Services, publication no. PEP19-5068 (August 2019). www.samhsa. gov/data/sites/default/files/cbhsq-reports/NSDUHNationalFindingsReport2018/ NSDUHNationalFindingsReport2018.pdf.

Schwartz, James L. 2010. "How to network." *GP Solo* 27, no 5.

Sciencio, Angelica. 2019. "You Should Try to Change What You Should Be Able to See." *The Practitioner* 25(1): 28–31.

Scott, Charity. 2018. "Mindfulness in Law: A Path to Wellbeing and Balance for Lawyers and Law Students." *Arizona Law Review* 60, no. 3: 35–171.

Seamone, Evan R. 2014. "Sex Crimes Litigation as Hazardous Duty: Practical Tools for Trauma-Exposed Prosecutors, Defense Counsel, and Paralegals. *Ohio State Journal of Criminal Law* 11, no. 2: 487–578.

Shapcott, Sue, Sarah Davis, and Lane Hanson. 2018. "The Jury Is In: Law schools Foster Students' Fixed Mindsets." *Law & Psychology Review* 42: 1–33. doi: 10.2139/ssrn.3236529.

Simmons, Richard. 2015. "Salary Survey: Stress." The Lawyer: Careers. https://jobs. thelawyer.com/article/salary-survey-stress/.

Simmons, Richard. 2018. "Firm Launches 'Panic Button' for Overworked Lawyers." *The Lawyer*. https://www.thelawyer.com/pusch-wahlig-panic-button-law/.

Skead, Natalie K., and Rogers, Shane L. 2014. "Stress, Anxiety and Depression in Law Students: How Students Behaviours Affect Student Wellbeing." *Monash University Law Review* 40, no. 2: 564–587.

State Bar of California. 2019. "State Bar Board of Trustees Hears First-Ever Report on Racial Disparities in Attorney Discipline." News Releases, November 14, 2019. http://www.calbar.ca.gov/About-Us/News/News-Releases/state-bar-board-of-trustees-hears-first-ever-report-on-racial-disparities-in-attorney-discipline.

State v. Moisant, 457 P.3d 1040 (2019).

State v. Switzer, 790 N.W.2d 433 (2010).

State v. Thompson, 652 N.W.2d 593 (2002).

Supreme Court Attorney Disciplinary Board v. Roush, 827 N.W.2d 711 (2013).

Sweeney, Michael. J. 2002. "Lawyers in Recovery Have Low Claim Rates!" Oregon Attorney Assistance Program. *In Sight,* no. 46.

Swenson, David, Joan Bibelhausen, Bree Buchanan, David Shaheed, and Katheryn Yetter for the American Bar Association Center for Professional Responsibility Publications Board. 2020. "Stress and Resilience in the U.S. Judiciary." *Journal of the Professional Lawyer*.

Tarascio, Billie. 2020. "Depression Among Lawyers: The Statistics." Modern Law Practice. modernlawpractice.com/depression-among-lawyers-the-statistics/.

Temple, Hollee Schwartz. 2012. "Speaking Up: Helping Law Students Break Through the Silence of Depression." *ABA Journal* 98, no. 2: 23–24.

Thangarasu, Sudhagar, Gowri Renganathan, and Piruthiviraj Natarajan. 2021. "Empathy Can Be Taught, and Patients Teach it Best." *Journal of Medical Education and Curricular Development* 8: 1–3. doi: 10.1177/23821205211000346.

Thomas, M. E. 2014. *Confessions of a Sociopath: A Life Spent Hiding in Plain Sight.* New York: Broadway Books.

Thomas, Philip W. 2017. "Law Firms Getting More Proactive in Addressing Attorney Mental Health. *MS Litigation Review & Commentary* (blog), May 30, 2017. www.mslitigationreview.com/2017/05/articles/attorney-mental-health/law-firms-getting-more-proactive-in-addressing-attorney-mental-health/.

Truant, G.S. 1999. "Assessment of Suitability for Psychotherapy." *American Journal of Psychotherapy* 53, no. 1: 17–34.

Tyler, Ronald. 2016. "The First Thing We Do, Let's Heal All the Law Students: Incorporating Self-Care into a Criminal Defense Clinic." *Berkeley Journal of Criminal Law* 21, no. 2: 1–34. doi: 10.15779/Z38KD1QJ9N.

U.S. Bureau of Labor Statistics. 2020. "Lawyers." *Occupational Outlook Handbook.* https://www.bls.gov/ooh/legal/lawyers.htm.

Velleman, Paul F. 2016. "Statistics Failures Make Lawyer Addiction Estimates Worthless." *American Society of Addiction Medicine* 10, no. 4 (July/August): 286–287. 10.1097/ADM.0000000000000226.

Vrklevski, Lila Petar, and John Franklin. 2008. "Vicarious Trauma: The Impact on Solicitors of Exposure to Traumatic Material." *Traumatology* 14, no. 1: 106–118. doi: 10.1177/1534765607309961.

Wait-O'Brien, Nancy. 2009. "Women: Overcoming Barriers to Treatment." Highlights Newsletter.

Weiss, Debra Cassens. 2020. "State Bar Takes 'Medieval Approach to Mental Health,' Says Trump-Appointed Judge. *ABA Journal*, September 1, 2020. www.abajournal.com/news/article/state-bar-takes-medieval-approach-to-mental-health-says-federal-judge.

Wernz, William. J. 1988. "Psychological Problems and Discipline." *Bench & Bar of Minnesota*. Reprint.

Wittchen, Hans-Ulrich, Stephan Mühlig, and Katja Beesdo. 2003. "Mental Disorders in Primary Care." *Dialogues in Clinical Neuroscience* 5, no. 2: 115–128.

Woods, Kathleen Guthrie. 2018. "Let's Lose the Booze: Rethinking Networking Events." *San Francisco Attorney* 34: 18.

Yale Law School. 2018. "The Truth About the Billable Hour. https://law.yale.edu/sites/default/files/area/department/cdo/document/billable_hour.pdf.

Zacharias, Fred C. 2003. "The Purposes of Lawyer Discipline." *William and Mary Law Review* 45, no. 2: 675–745. https://scholarship.law.wm.edu/wmlr/vol45/iss2/6.

Zaidi, Lisa Y., and David W. Foy. 1994. "Childhood Abuse Experiences and Combat-Related PTSD." *Journal of Traumatic Stress* 7: 33–42. doi 10.1007/BF02111910.

Zimmerman, Eilene. 2020. "A Widow, Not a Wife: 'Smacked' Explores an Ex-Husband's Secret Addiction." Interview by Terry Gross. *Fresh Air*, NPR, February 4, 2020. Audio, 36:00. www.npr.org/sections/health-shots/2020/02/04/802479660/a-widow-not-a-wife-smacked-explores-an-ex-husbands-secret-addiction.

Index

About the Authors

Catherine Young, JD, PhD is licensed California attorney and clinical psychologist. She earned her law degree from Southwestern Law School and her PhD in Clinical Psychology at Palo Alto University. Her primary clinical interests are correctional psychology and psychoanalysis.

Wendy Packman, JD, PhD is professor emerita of psychology at Palo Alto University (PAU) and the Director, Emerita of the Joint JD-PhD Program in Psychology and Law at PAU and Golden Gate University Law School. Her research interests/publications in psychology and the law include ethical and legal issues in child and pediatric psychology, risk management with suicidal patients, and malpractice. Dr. Packman has studied, presented, and written extensively on sibling bereavement and continuing bonds, the impact of a child's death on parents, and the psychological sequelae of pet loss.